RIDING THE
BEAR

RIDING THE BEAR

How to Prosper in the Coming Bear Market

Sy Harding

Adams Media Corporation
Avon, Massachusetts

Published by
Adams Media Corporation
57 Littlefield Street, Avon, MA 02322. U.S.A.
www.adamsmedia.com

ISBN: 1-58062-154-6

Printed in the United States of America.

J I H G F

Library of Congress Cataloging-in-Publication Data
Harding, Sy.
Riding the bear : reap huge gains in Bull and Bear markets! / Sy Harding.
p.   cm.
ISBN 1-58062-154-6
1. Investments—United States. 2. Stock exchanges—United States. I. Title.
HG4910.H37   1999
332.63'2—dc21   98-54701
CIP

This publication is designed to provide accurate and authoritative information with
regard to the subject matter covered. It is sold with the understanding that the
publisher is not engaged in rendering legal, accounting, or other professional advice.
If legal advice or other expert assistance is required, the services of a competent
professional person should be sought.
— From a *Declaration of Principles* jointly adopted by a Committee of the
American Bar Association and a Committee of Publishers and Associations

Charts on pages 36 and 95 courtesy of Ned Davis Research, Inc.
All other charts courtesy of Asset Management Research Corp.

Cover photo ©1998 Ron Sanford/Alaska Stock Images.

This book is available at quantity discounts for bulk purchases.
For information, call 1-800-872-5627.

*To my wife, Dale Stewart Harding, whose faith
in this work kept me going on it while keeping me always
aware of the true values in life and the need to stop
and smell the roses.*

*To my three children, Linda, Jeff, and Patti,
each of whom has shown me so much about what
is important in life. I am so proud of you,
and love you all so very much.*

*To my ex-wife, friend, and business associate,
Phyllis Harding, a first-class lady.*

CONTENTS

ACKNOWLEDGMENTS

I'd like to thank those whose contributions made this book possible:

My wife, Dale, whose ability to guide me away from the abstruseness of economic and market jargon added to the book's readability.

My son, and business partner, Jeff, whose insights into the market, and ability with computers and programming, added so much to the studies and back-testing of data.

My agent, Chris Byrne, at Harold Ober Associates, for recognition of the value of *Riding the Bear* to investors, and ability to choose a publisher that could, and would, respond with the required urgency.

My publisher, Adams Media, for its enthusiasm for the project, and to my editor, Jere Calmes, for his motivating guidance.

I'd also like to thank those whose prior work and data I drew on to help make my points;

Ned Davis
Ned Davis Research Group
2100 Riveredge Parkway, Suite 750
Atlanta, GA 30328

Norman G. Fosback
Institute for Econometric Research
2200 S.W. 10th Street
Deerfield Beach, FL 33442

Michael L. Burke
Investors Intelligence
30 Church Street
New Rochelle, NY 10801

Yale Hirsch
The Hirsch Organization Inc.
184 Central Ave.
Old Tappen, NJ 07675

I'd also like to acknowledge the investigative reporters of *Barron's*, *Business Week*, *Forbes*, *Fortune*, *The Wall Street Journal*, and *Investor's Business Daily*, who are not afraid to tell it like it is and whose articles often steered me toward important information.

It's important that the following information become public knowledge!
When you finish reading this book, please send or recommend it to friends, family members, anyone you care about, that has assets at risk in the stock market, assets that are subject to either devastating losses, or huge gains. Help us get out the word about this book's value to investors on the Internet and in investment clubs.

And since business will have its floods and ebbs, and the spirit of enterprise and production must be checked for a time, the more promptly the approaching crises can be seen and provided against, as far as practicable, the less the community will suffer.

William Phillips, 1828

PREFACE

Why do statistics show that while temporarily successful in bull markets, over the long term, 80 percent of investors either lose money in the stock market or fail to beat the gain they would make by simply leaving their money in the bank?

By the time you finish this book, you're going to know why. You're going to have a lot of knowledge you don't have now. You're going to be a much wiser investor than you are now. *You're going to be able to make much larger profits from the market, and keep them.*

You're going to hear things you've never heard before, and are unlikely to hear again. For the most part, the only people in a position to tell you these things, *won't* tell you because they are the very people whose financial success depends on public investors remaining misinformed.

It's most important for current investors to have this information since the unprecedented surge in the bull market of the 1990s has excited and enticed investors as never before in history. The stock market has become a national obsession. In their excitement, many investors believe they've discovered something new, a perpetual-motion money-making machine. The ease with which profits have been made has combined forces with the salesmanship of Wall Street to convince investors of that.

However, the stock market is not something new. It's been around for 200 years. It's definitely not an endless money-making machine, but can produce both gains or losses.

Except for the last nine years, a devastating bear market has always struck at investors' portfolios on average of every three years. Few investors emerge financially intact from such experiences. Yet hardly any of today's investors are prepared for the inevitability that *they* will also periodically endure such potentially devastating experiences. As has always been the case, how they prepare for and handle those experiences, not how much they make in bull markets, will determine whether or not they make gains in the long run, or fall into the category of the majority of public investors, who over the long run lose money in the market.

Riding the Bear is aimed at ending the vicious cycle for its readers. It is not aimed at market professionals and corporate insiders, who *know* what's going on, but at public investors that Wall Street so successfully trains to buy high and sell low, while Wall Street takes the opposite side of the public's activity, buying low and selling high.

Our goal was to write in plain English and avoid the extended economic and statistical analysis of academia that so understandably causes investors' eyes to glaze over.

However, you *will* learn the forces that keep both bull and bear markets going to extremes, why bull markets have such an easy time convincing investors they will last forever, while bear markets have an equally easy time convincing investors that good times will not return in their lifetimes.

You will not only learn how to get on the right side of the cycle and stay there, but how to harness the power of *both* bull and bear markets to your own advantage.

We believe you will find this wake-up call to investors a fascinating journey that will forever change the way you approach investing.

CHAPTER 1

BEARS ARE TOOTHLESS NOW? DON'T YOU BELIEVE IT!

Over the last 100 years, there have been 29 serious stock market corrections, or bear markets, *one on average every 3.3 years*, with declines averaging 31.6 percent. There were ten in which the declines averaged 49.4 percent. In those, investors lost half of their invested assets. Yet in the upside of every cycle, the endurance of the bull market transports investors into a state of confidence where they believe this time will be different.

The record-breaking bull market of the 1990s certainly has had that effect, the excitement sweeping investors into the market as never before, their easy profits then carrying them away on a euphoric wave of confidence that they've discovered something new, a risk-free money machine—and it never breaks down.

Self-serving brokerage firm and mutual fund spokespeople, anxious to keep new money flowing in, tell investors their expectations are on the mark. "It's a new era. We won't have a bear market in stocks or a recession in the economy until well into the next century, if then."

Their story sounds true and convincing, and it became the main support for continuing investor confidence.

Wall Street tells investors that bear markets took place "in the old days," back when the robber barons were manipulating the market, when the economy cycled back and forth between boom times and recessions, before the Federal Reserve learned how to keep everything on an even keel. They took place back when almost everyone worked in factories, whereas now more than half the population works in the service industry. Factories lay off workers when inventories get too high, or the factory becomes obsolete, or a competitor buys them out. But the service industry just keeps going and growing, taking advantage of the way lifestyles are changing.

They tell investors the proof is all around them. Large, old-style companies have had bigger layoffs than ever in recent years because of so-called restructuring and downsizing, but it isn't causing the slightest hiccup in the economy, where the unemployment rate is at its lowest level since Eisenhower was president. New, rapidly growing high-tech companies take up the slack as old-style companies lay off workers, and the economy just keeps rolling along.

Wall Street's story is that a technological revolution has taken place. Computers and automation allow even old-style businesses to become more productive with ever-fewer employees. Therefore, corporate earnings will grow well into the next decade. Even the products of factories are changing, they point out. High-tech products from computers to biotech medical miracles are in their infancy, destined to grow for generations. Inflation is low. Interest rates are low. They call it a "Goldilocks" economy, neither too hot nor too cold, but just right for another decade of booming stock market. The cycle of bull markets and bear markets will not be seen again in our lifetimes.

Ominously, Yale economist Robert Shiller, who has studied the history of investor behavior more closely than probably anyone, notes the similarity to investor euphoria in 1929. In the 1920s, the supreme confidence that the good times could go on forever was also based on a momentous technological breakthrough, the introduction of electricity into everyday living, a change even more revolutionary than that brought about by computers in the 1990s. The huge boost in productivity brought about by factories being run by electricity, and new modern production methods, including Henry Ford's introduction of the assembly line, allowed fewer employees to produce increasingly more products. A continuous stream of new electric products for homes and businesses had new growth companies popping up everywhere. The assembly line made automobiles affordable for everyone. Studebaker, Packard, Standard Oil, RKO Studios, RCA, Westinghouse, Marconi, and dozens of others were the Microsofts, Intels, and Yahoos of that bull market. John D. Rockefeller and Joseph P. Kennedy, one an industry builder, the other a sharp investor, were the Bill Gates and Warren Buffett of the times. Everyone believed it. The economy, and thus the stock market, could continue growing without pause for many decades.

Unfortunately, the theory was almost immediately destroyed when the 1929 stock market crash followed. The bull market of the 1920s, which *at that time* had also been the longest and most consistently profitable bull market ever, having lasted eight years, quickly plunged into the worst bear market ever. The stock market lost 86 percent of its value over the following three years. The strongest economic cycle ever, which was supposedly destined to continue for decades, reversed to the worst recession ever seen, the Great Depression.

That's the way it's been for the entire 200 years of the stock market's existence. The stock market cycles between bull markets and bear markets on a fairly consistent basis.

Unfortunately, the reversals in both directions take place just when public investors have become convinced the current market direction will continue forever, and have their portfolios positioned on that expectation. In a bull market, the endlessly rising stock prices and easy profits move investor sentiment to an extreme of euphoria and confidence. Thoughts of risk are brushed aside. Unreasonable expectations prevail. Theories of why this time will be different—this time the bull market *can* last forever—become gospel.

Bear markets progress to the opposite extreme. Once they begin, they don't end until doom and gloom are at an extreme, until investors and the media have become convinced that good times will never return, until the last "buy and hold" investor has sold—and sworn off "the damned market" for good.

Such is the way it is—every time. We don't have to theorize about it. Nowhere are there more accurate statistical records than in the stock market.

Let's take a brief look. The following table shows all the serious "corrections" or bear markets of the last 100 years. Investors, convinced that the market rarely suffers more than a brief 10 or 15 percent "pullback," would do well to study the table for a few minutes.

MARKET TOP	MARKET LOW	DECLINE	MARKET TOP	MARKET LOW	DECLINE	MARKET TOP	MARKET LOW	DECLINE
06/17/01	11/09/03	-41%	02/05/34	07/26/34	-22.8%	12/03/68	05/26/70	-35.9%
01/19/06	11/15/07	-48.5%	03/10/37	03/31/38	-49.1%	04/28/71	11/23/71	-16.1%
11/19/09	09/25/11	-27.4%	11/12/38	04/08/39	-23.3%	01/11/73	12/06/74	-45.1%
09/30/12	07/30/14	-24.1%	09/12/39	04/28/42	-40.4%	09/21/76	02/28/78	-26.9%
11/21/16	12/19/17	-40.1%	05/29/46	05/17/47	-23.2%	09/08/78	04/21/80	-16.4%
11/03/19	08/24/21	-46.6%	06/15/48	06/13/49	-16.3%	04/27/81	08/12/82	-24.1%
03/20/23	10/27/23	-18.6%	04/06/56	10/22/57	-19.4%	11/29/83	07/24/84	-15.6%
09/03/29	11/13/29	-47.9%	01/05/60	10/25/60	-17.4%	08/25/87	10/19/87	-36.1%
04/17/30	07/08/32	-86.0%	12/13/61	06/26/62	-27.1%	07/16/90	10/11/90	-21.2%
09/07/32	02/27/33	-37.2%	02/09/66	10/07/66	-25.2%			

Note that over the past 100 years there have been 29 bear markets, *one on average every 3.3 years*. The declines averaged 31.6 percent. *The nine worst bear markets wiped out an average of 49.4 percent of stock market value*, and one of those puppies came along every ten years or so.

Note also that though most investors believe that bear markets were a phenomenon of the old days, the fact is that bear markets have taken place more frequently in modern times. The last ten bear markets took place an average of one *every 2.4 years*, averaging a decline of 29 percent.

We're obviously talking about significant declines, frequent and devastating intervals for the typical investor. It's the public's failure to understand or handle the periodic bear markets that produces the discouraging statistic that over the long term the majority of public investors either lose money in the stock market or fail to beat the gain they would make by simply leaving their money in the bank.

CHAPTER 2

EXTENDING TRENDS TO INFINITY

Bull markets have an easy task of enticing every last dollar in near the top. Bear markets have an equally easy task of convincing investors to then bail out at the bear market low, with devastating losses. Both forces stem from the practice of mentally extending current trends into infinity, the favorite forecasting tool of scientists and economists, as well as investors.

The delusion of such thinking is best illustrated by the fact that the world hardly ever comes to an end. Yet for centuries "trend extending" has regularly predicted just such a result—based on everything from holy wars, black plague, and rising ocean levels, centuries ago, to nuclear weapons, depleting ozone layer, global warming, and communism taking over the world, of more recent times. In the 1940s, it was scientific fact that there would not be enough land to feed the growing U.S. population by the year 2000.

However, trends continue only until conditions change.

Farmers learn new soil management, new cattle feeding and breeding techniques. Science develops healthier seeds. Farm machinery manufacturers provide more efficient equipment. Oblivion is not only avoided and the trend reversed, but the problem cycles to the opposite extreme: food surpluses, overflowing government food warehouses, gifts of surplus grains to foreign countries, even subsidies to farmers to leave their fields unplanted.

Cures are discovered for the most devastating of diseases, with the result that the straight-line trend to extinction is not only halted, but reversed to ever-longer life expectancies. Not surprisingly, that new trend is then extended in a straight line in the opposite direction, to a fear that ever-longer life expectancies will bankrupt the Social Security system, and ever-older but healthier elders will drastically change the world in previously unimaginable ways.

Communism spreads across half the planet, raising a real concern that it will eventually take over the rest of the world, but in the process stretches its untenable economics past the limit, and the trend reverses to the present expectation that communism is headed to oblivion. (Don't bet on it.)

However, nowhere is the tendency to extend trends in a straight line, without expectation of reversals, more prevalent than in the world of investing.

Infamous historical events like the "Tulip Bulb Mania," the "South Sea Bubble," the Florida Land Crash, even the 1929 stock market crash are examples of "this time is different" trends turning around to bite investors savagely. However, they were extreme, and rare, in that they *totally* wiped investors out. They're also easy to shrug off as old-time events.

Unfortunately, more recent events demonstrate that nothing has changed to lower the eventual cost to investors of thinking trends rather than cycles. Let's look at a few examples.

CALIFORNIA, HERE WE COME

By the early 1980s, it seemed to have become everyone's dream to live in California. Nice weather. Low crime rate. Plentiful jobs. Low taxes. The westward continental drift was soon being compared to wagon train days and created demand for housing in California that significantly exceeded the supply. Real estate prices began rising 25 percent per year and more. Property owners and early developers made fortunes that were well publicized. Not surprisingly, get-rich-quick advice soon followed, pointing out how easily ordinary folk could get in on the action.

Middle-income families, with no knowledge of the economics of real estate investments or the dangers of leverage, began taking second mortgages on their homes, using the proceeds as minimum down payments on any property, at any price. It didn't matter if they overpaid. The way prices were rising, they'd make big profits anyway. As soon as a newly acquired property rose 10 percent in value, the strategy was to take that extra equity out in the form of a second mortgage and use it as a down payment on yet another property. Banks loved it. "Paper" millionaires were everywhere. The process was indeed working for everyone.

Optimism became so extreme that in some areas small crowds gathered at real estate offices, where brokers held lotteries to determine who would be allowed to pay the exorbitant price of the next new listing to come in. Bidding wars broke out where sellers were offered substantial premiums above their asking price. Buyers were signing contracts to build a new house, and the *contract* was being sold and resold several times, each time at a profit, before the house was even completed.

No one was thinking cycles. The trend of sharply rising prices was being extended in a straight line that seemingly would never end. Warnings of an unsustainable "bubble" forming in prices, and signs that some professionals were taking their profits and standing aside, were ridiculed by participants. With the obvious demand, how could prices possibly stop rising—ever.

Alas, just as it began to appear that perhaps they were right—that this time was somehow different—the trend turned on them with a vengeance.

Skyrocketing real estate taxes and insurance costs had become a problem for everyone, but particularly for those who were holding extra properties on a shoestring of equity while waiting for them to appreciate in value. A series of televised earthquakes, mudslides, and wildfires slowed the westward drift of outsiders. Horror of horrors, even longtime Californians began putting their homes on the market so they could move out—to the low-cost and newly perceived paradises of Oregon, Nevada, and Colorado.

The California real estate market was soon a catastrophe. For sale signs lingered on properties, with few buyers in sight. Sellers began to drop prices quickly, seeing themselves in a race to get out fast before prices fell further. Developers, who had grossly overproduced to meet a demand they expected to grow forever, were stuck with huge inventories of unsold homes on which they couldn't pay the mortgages. Bankruptcy was their only option. Banks threw foreclosed properties on the market at fire-sale prices, plunging real estate prices even further.

Individual investors discovered that the magic of leverage that had compounded their paper gains so excitingly when prices were rising now leveraged their losses. Since they had made just 10 percent down payments, by the time their properties declined just 15 percent in value, they had lost 100 percent of their investment. Most simply walked away from their mortgages, leaving the banks holding the bag. Within a year, California real estate prices had plunged 35 percent and more. Ten years later, they were just beginning to recover.

Only those who heeded the warnings, curbed their greed, and took their profits as the top approached kept their big gains and were ready to invest in the early stages of the next cycle.

JAPAN: THE RISING SUN ALSO EVENTUALLY SETS

In the late 1980s, as stock markets around the world soared toward the October 1987 crash, the Japanese stock market was one of the biggest winners. In the crash, the U.S. market lost 36 percent of its value in three months, but the Japanese market declined only 18 percent and immediately began to soar again, outperforming every market in sight. Institutions around the world, encouraged by the Japanese market's resilience, began to pour assets into it, driving an already overvalued market ever higher. Small investors, particularly in Japan, but also around the world, belatedly caught the excitement, and began to pour *their* savings into Japanese stocks as never before in history.

The Japanese market became a true mania. The Japanese population, traditionally savers and investors in real estate, wound up by 1989 with by far the largest percentage ever of their assets in the stock market. It was an easy game in which the profits were quick and large, and seemingly endless. Japanese housewives were being told they could join the ranks of the wealthy if they would simply use a portion of their household allowance to make regular monthly purchases in the stock market, "averaging in." The excitement was epidemic.

Investors laughed off warnings that stocks were selling at unsustainable multiples of earnings and dividend yields as the fears of an older generation, confidently exclaiming that "this time is different" and "dividends no longer matter."

Japanese banks and investment companies, caught up in the giddiness, used their huge gains to swarm around the world, particularly the United States, buying up landmark properties, from Pebble Beach Golf Club to Rockefeller Center. They paid prices no one else could justify or afford, flush with paper profits from the booming Japanese stock market. If you recall, it reached the point that economists and Congress were alarmed that Japan, having lost World War II, might wind up winning after all, by buying and controlling major U.S. assets.

However, three years later in 1990, when stock markets around the world suffered their next, and mercifully brief, bear market, the Japanese market did not prove to be the safer haven.

As the chart shows, the Japanese Nikkei plunged 65 percent from its peak in 1989 to its low in 1992 and, in spite of numerous rallies, remained 65 percent below that peak nine years later. Again, only those who heeded the early warnings made out well, by curbing their greed, realizing the inevitability of cycles, and taking their profits early. Those who fell for the brokerage firm advice to simply buy and hold because "the market always comes back," are still waiting.

By 1992, Japanese institutions were circling the globe again, this time selling off at fire-sale prices the choice properties they

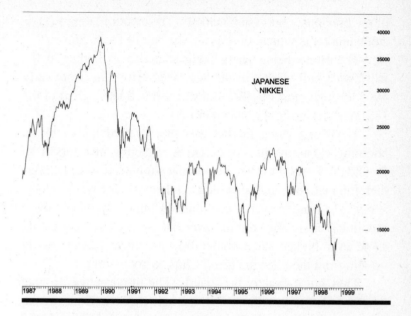

had so recently bought at exorbitant prices. They needed to raise cash to survive their horrible stock market losses. For many, it was too late. Bankruptcies soared, and Japan has been mired in a long and deep recession since then.

Not only did the trend in the Japanese stock market reverse direction and move to the opposite extreme, but so also did Japanese consumer confidence. Japanese consumers, burned by their previous overconfidence in the stock market, and much poorer for the experience, returned to being savers to a dramatic degree. Economists have labored unsuccessfully for almost a decade now trying to come up with a plan to encourage fearful Japanese consumers to stop hoarding cash. The Japanese economy cannot emerge from its long economic recession until Japanese consumer confidence returns and consumers begin buying the products of their corporations again.

THE HONG KONG FLU

Even more recent proof that market cycles have not been replaced by endless trends can be seen in the 1997–1998 action of the previously hot Asian markets. The chart of Hong Kong's stock market is typical of those in the rest of the region.

The Hong Kong Hang Seng soared ever higher in the worldwide bull market of the late 1990s. (Its chart from early 1995 through most of 1997 looks very much like a chart of the U.S. market during the same period.)

The Hong Kong market was first spurred higher by its booming economy, its stock market attracting investors from around the world. In 1997, after a brief stumble, it spiked up further. International analysts predicted this former British colony, about to be handed over to communist China, would experience a political crisis after the turnover but its stock market would surge ever higher since bottled-up investment money would flow in from the huge mainland Chinese population.

They got it exactly backwards. The turnover was trouble free politically, but the stock market crashed. Once again, cycles proved more important than trends. The Hong Kong stock market plunged 46 percent in three months. By mid-1998, it was down 56 percent. Investors had lost virtually all of their gains from the exciting previous three years.

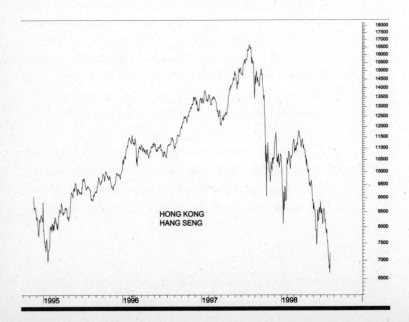

Similar serious bear markets began in 1997 in most other Asian countries, including Thailand, Indonesia, Malaysia, Singapore, South Korea, and the Philippines. Their economies, which were so persistently strong and seemingly unstoppable in early 1997 that they were known as the Asian "tiger" economies, seemingly fell off a precipice. Their currencies plummeted. Their stock markets plunged more than 50 percent. Their economies fell into recession. Their substantial middle-class populace was increasingly pushed back into poverty. Riots in 1998 over the scarcity of food and jobs toppled the government in Thailand, and came close to doing so in South Korea. Massive financial aid had to be rushed into the region from the International Monetary Fund.

What had happened? The strong Asian "tiger" economies had attracted so much investment money, much of which was poured into new production facilities, that soon there were more factories and office buildings than there was available business. Extending the trend, rather than thinking cycles, developers and other astute businesspeople thought business demand would continue rising endlessly and would be there to occupy new factories and skyscrapers when they were completed. Instead, idle and empty factories and office buildings soon dotted the landscape, commercial real estate prices plunged, banks suffered, the stock market plunged, the bubble burst.

RUSSIA: COMRADE, WHAT IS THIS THING, INCOME TAXES?

In the mid-1990s, the rush to capitalism in Russia, including privatization of previously state-owned industry, and the introduction of a stock market, was greeted with great enthusiasm by investors around the world. Once released from the heavy burden of management by decree, powered by the rocket fuel of free enterprise, how could the Russian economy not explode upward? An avalanche of money poured into the newly created stocks of Russian companies. Brokerage firms ecstatically began extending a trend they claimed would last for decades.

Alas, the path more closely resembled the flight of a Roman candle. By late 1998, the Russian stock market had crashed and burned, having plummeted 85 percent from its 1997 peak. The Russian economy was in such a mess its very survival was suddenly in question.

What had happened? Basically, the Russian people did not fully comprehend capitalism and were not prepared for its requirements. Many could not understand why the government was no longer taking care of all of their needs, whereas others interpreted the freedom to pursue profits as a license for mafia-like business tactics that scared off badly needed foreign business relationships. One of the biggest misunderstandings involved the need to pay income taxes once the government no longer directly received the revenues of industry. Many Russian individuals and businesses simply would not pay, bringing the government close to total collapse.

All this is by means of saying that no matter how real an uptrend in prices or demand in anything—whether real estate, baseball cards, Cabbage Patch dolls, Beanie Babies, gold Krugerands, or stocks—*trends do end. Prices cannot grow to the sky. Demand cannot rise endlessly. Rising trends will* always *ultimately create extreme conditions that guarantee their reversal.*

GREED AND FEAR

It's important to realize that as the stock market cycles back and forth between bull markets and bear markets, investor psychology cycles back and forth between extremes of greed and extremes of fear, and it's those *emotions* that move the market to extremes in both directions.

The psychological reversals are easy enough to understand.

In bull markets, the gains are exciting and intoxicating. It's great fun to constantly check the market to see how much money is being made. It's great fun to talk about the markets and stocks and those big profits with others. It's all so easy, and a real high, to discover that there really is a quick way to get rich. What fun to daydream about how soon the big gains will compound into a fortune that will allow exciting lifestyle changes— a larger home, a Porsche in the garage, early retirement. The stock market becomes an obsession, the subject of conversations around the dinner table, at cocktail parties, around the water cooler, and at the hairdressers. It's just great fun. The excitement and greed grow until even conservative "savers" have run out of cash and are remortgaging homes and borrowing against life insurance policies in order to raise more money for the market.

THE OTHER SIDE OF THE CYCLE

However, comes the inevitable bear market that history clearly tells us every investor must encounter on a fairly regular basis. Suddenly, the stock market is no fun at all. It is in fact incredibly painful and fear inducing to see previous gains disappear so rapidly. Soon there's no joy in discussing the miserable market with anyone. It's even embarrassing to admit being involved in it. The previous daydreams become nightmares. The previous euphoria becomes despair.

Eventually, even those who had determined that *this time* they would definitely be buy and hold investors because the market always comes back, give up on the strategy when the media and analysts finally stop talking of recovery, and begin extending this new trend in a straight line *down*, issuing plausible theories of why this time the *downside* is different, and a recovery may not be seen in our lifetimes. Then, even the determined buy and hold investors begin to sell, driving the market even lower.

Disillusionment among public investors then becomes so pervasive that long after the bear market has bottomed and the next bull market is underway, they want nothing to do with it. Only when the market gets back to its previous highs and goes on to new highs, creating excitement in the media, does their courage return.

Thus do they perpetuate their historical pattern of buying high and selling low, and contribute to the discouraging statistic that, over time, the vast majority of public investors lose money in the market.

The first step in breaking the devastating pattern—to wind up utilizing bull market–bear market cycles to profitable advantage—is acquiring knowledge: of the cycles, of the alternatives, of how to handle the powerful propaganda from Wall Street.

CHAPTER 3

RIDING THE STOCK MARKET RIVER

If you remember nothing else, remember this.

Stock or mutual fund selection is not nearly as important to your success in the stock market as is the direction of the overall market. Statistics show that when the market moves strongly *in either direction*, it carries roughly 75 percent of stocks with it. Only 25 percent *at most* will act counter to the underlying trend.

Therefore, even though your stock or mutual fund selection is superb, if the underlying market direction is down, as in a bear market, the odds are great that you will watch your good stocks go down because of the market decline, rather than see them go up because of their own merits.

In the other direction, even if your stock selection is horrible, if the underlying market is in a strong up move, as in a bull market, chances are even your poorest stock selections will be swept up with it. It's this marvelous wonder of even the poorest stocks being pulled up by a bull market that gives rise to the adage that "there's nothing like a bull market to make everyone believe they are an investing genius."

Investors *have* to understand the phenomenon. Otherwise, they become believers of the brokerage firm propaganda that as long as they select good stocks or mutual funds, they will not be adversely affected by bear markets.

HOW IS IT POSSIBLE?

How can bad stocks be lifted by a rising market, making investing in stocks look so easy? How can even good stocks, in companies with still-growing earnings and excellent futures, be pulled down in a bear market?

Imagine the stock market as a broad river flowing calmly through your town or city. As it flows gently along, with little underlying current, only those items that float well and are in the main stream go along with it. Small and large boats have no problem. Even a few solid boards that dream of being boats may be carried along. However, when the river is periodically flooded by volumes of additional water pouring in, from torrential rains or melting snow perhaps, it gains momentum, moves along more forcefully, and begins to sweep up less buoyant objects from the bottom and the riverbank. Fallen branches, pieces of water-logged wood that normally would not float, debris, yes, even garbage, are swept up and carried along.

However, on its endless journey to the sea, when the river subsequently comes to a waterfall where the entire river plunges to lower levels, everything in the river, good boats and garbage, if still in the river, are going to go down to the lower levels with it. Some will not even survive the plunge.

SO IT IS WITH THE STOCK MARKET

A bull market with strong upside momentum, created by a big inflow of new money flowing into it, carries even bad stocks up with it, whereas a bear market, dropping down to lower levels, carries even good stocks down with it.

What causes even bad stocks to rise in a bull market? There's only one force that causes a stock's price to rise, and that is increased investor demand for it, so-called buying pressure.

Why would investors' demand for *bad* stocks increase just because a bull market is underway? It works like this.

When a new bull market begins, understandably the best stocks attract the first buying, and are driven up. But as the rising market entices increasingly more participants, and the best stocks become more expensive, a search begins for good stocks that have been overlooked. They may not be the best, but with the best already getting pricey, the next to best begin to look more attractive. So money begins to also flow into those good, but less than best, stocks, driving *them* higher. As that happens, investors (and stock brokers) become more confident, and in their search for stocks that have yet to participate, move increasingly into stocks of lesser quality, causing even those stocks to rise in price.

Eventually, as the market soars higher, confidence becomes high that virtually any stock, bought at any price, will be a winner, with the result that any stock on which stock promoters can cook up a "story," even garbage stocks, will attract buying. Thus do even bad stocks eventually participate in bull markets.

Okay. That's understandable. But how can even good stocks, with continuing earnings growth, be pulled down in a bear market?

THE WATERFALL EFFECT OF A BEAR MARKET

As the market *begins* to decline into what will become a full-fledged bear market, investors are usually unconcerned. Their only experience has been with the endlessly rising bull market, which with its brief 10 or 15 percent pullbacks, has trained them to believe that all market declines will just be further buying opportunities.

As the decline worsens, they become increasingly nervous, but Wall Street assures them that all will be well. It might be a little more severe than previous pullbacks, but there's no reason to believe the bull market has ended. And sure enough, there are occasional brief bounces that relieve investors' concerns.

However, a change has taken place. Now, each time the market attempts to rally again, it soon fails, and the decline resumes.

As this new pattern of brief failing rallies, followed by lower lows, repeats and investors' portfolios continue to plunge, fear takes over, and then panic. In an effort to stem their losses, investors sell holdings with increased frenzy and, as the cliché goes, throw the baby out with the bath water. It's well documented that most individual investors have the attitude that, although a stock may have lost half its value "on paper," they have not suffered a loss until they actually sell the stock. Therefore, reluctant to take losses, but determined to reduce their exposure to the declining market, they sell their best stocks first, those on which they still have profits or on which the losses are smaller. Only later, when totally panicked, will they also sell their worst holdings, those with the largest losses.

Thus do even good stocks see their prices collapse when the market goes over the bear market waterfall.

MUTUAL FUNDS NAVIGATE ON THE SAME RIVER

Many investors are under the impression that since their money is in mutual funds, it's not at the same risk in a bear market decline. They assume it's the fund manager's job to engage in some form of risk management so as to protect them from changing market conditions. *They could not be more mistaken.*

Every mutual fund is managed in accordance with the mandate of its specific prospectus. A fund that's advertised as investing in technology stocks does just that. A fund that's set up to invest in growth-type stocks confines itself to such stocks. A fund set up to be diversified among emerging country stocks will limit itself to those investments. That *must* be. Investors have chosen the fund's particular strategy for their assets and are depending on the fund not deviating from the strategy. Therefore, for instance, even if the manager of a fund that invests in small capitalization stocks believes such stocks are headed into a prolonged period of declining prices, and that large capitalization stocks will be substantial winners, he or she cannot, and will not, deviate from the fund's mandate to invest only in small stocks.

Further, a mutual fund will almost always be *fully invested* in its mandated strategy. Although the manager may frequently buy and sell individual stocks for the fund, he or she will usually keep the fund fully invested. Same reason. An investor who decides to be 60 percent invested in stocks and 40 percent in cash has to know that when he or she sends 60 percent of his or her money to a selected mutual fund it will all be invested. If the mutual fund manager were to decide that market risk is too high, and moved the fund to only 50 percent invested, the investor would unknowingly be only 30 percent invested.

The result is that asset allocation decisions—including how much exposure to the market an investor should have at any particular time—are not the responsibility of the investor's mutual fund managers, but are solely the responsibility of the investor.

That's not necessarily a bad thing, as long as investors realize the task is in their hands. Unfortunately, many do not, and in a prolonged bear market will be disappointed, to say the least, to learn that their mutual fund was riding on that same stock market river.

CHAPTER 4

WHAT CAUSES BEAR MARKETS ANYWAY?

In a word—excesses.

A new investor once wrote me to ask what I meant by the term *market correction*. What is it that the market is *correcting* when it declines, she wanted to know.

The answer, of course, is it's correcting the excesses created by the previous bull market. The almost uncontrolled frenzy to own stocks at any price, which takes place as a bull market matures, boosts stock prices to unreasonable levels related to the value of the company the stock represents. The euphoria causes investors to lose touch with reality and commit an excessive portion of their assets and future security to the vagaries of the market. Those overvalued and overbought extremes eventually become unsustainable and have to be "corrected."

Who says so? Why can't people just keep buying? Why can't the market just keep rising? Why does it have to become unsustainable?

For one thing, because the higher the market rises, the more new money it requires to keep it rising, while the more money investors put in the market, the closer they come to running out of money.

Think back to our analogy of the stock market being like a flowing river. As the river, being flooded by melting snows and torrential rains, grows ever wider and deeper, it must have an increasingly larger volume of additional water flowing in to *keep* it rising. It takes twice as much additional water to raise a 100-foot-wide river another 24 inches as it took when it was only 50 feet wide. If the inflow of water does not continue to *grow*, the river will stop rising. If the inflow of new water *decreases* to any degree at all, the high-water conditions will begin to recede. From years of experience, everyone knows the rising river cannot continue rising forever. There is only so much snow to melt.

So it is with the stock market. The higher the market rises, the more new money must flow in to keep it rising. It takes twice as much new money to raise the value of a $4 trillion market 10 percent, as it took to raise it 10 percent when it was only a $2 trillion market.

Yet, investors also have only so much melting snow available. They scramble around to find more, but eventually they are fully invested, and there just is no more, or at least not enough more to even sustain the current high level of inflow, let alone enough to keep that inflow increasing. The market's rise has become unsustainable.

SUPPLY AND DEMAND FORCES

The stock market is driven by the same forces of supply and demand that control any free market. As long as demand for a product (or a stock) exceeds the supply, higher prices can be demanded and will be paid. However, if something happens that either increases supply or decreases demand, sellers will have to lower prices in order to entice enough buyers.

The supply–demand equation is obvious in a bear market when everyone is trying to get out of harm's way by selling their holdings, and few investors are willing to step in with any degree of buying. The supply of stocks obviously overwhelms the demand, and prices seem to drop into a bottomless pit. Hundreds of billions of dollars of valuation simply disappear.

The effect of the supply–demand equation is also obvious in a bull market, when investors, willing to buy any stock at any price, and operating out of fear of being left behind by a rising market, provide tremendous demand for stocks, at the same time that holders of stocks are reluctant to sell because prices are rising. Obviously, the buyers have to pay ever-higher prices in order to entice some of the sellers to sell.

Another important but less obvious change in the supply–demand equation takes place on the supply side, as a bull market matures. More and more owners of privately owned companies, enticed by the high prices being paid for publicly traded companies, decide to sell all or part of their company to the public via an "initial public offering," or IPO. The longer a bull market lasts, and the more stock prices become out of whack with the underlying value of companies, the more privately owned companies are enticed to "go public."

In addition to IPOs, as a bull market matures, existing public companies are enticed to take advantage of the high prices by issuing more shares of their stock to the public.

Every $100 million of investor money that goes into new stock is $100 million that is not available to drive existing stocks higher. The rising river is finding new branches to send the inflow of water down, which will slow the rise in the main river.

So, as a bull market matures, supply factors are already working toward producing the inevitable bear market that will follow, at the same time that investors increasingly approach fully invested levels where they will have less new money to keep demand rising.

SENDING IT OVER THE WATERFALL

Once the market reaches the condition where investors *are* pretty much fully invested, and stock prices are at extremes of overvaluation, already tempting some to begin taking profits, all that's needed is a catalyst that raises doubts about the euphoria that's been supporting the market, and it's ready to roll over the top.

Historically, the most frequent catalyst has been an upside reversal in interest rates, as the Federal Reserve taps on the brakes to slow the booming economy that usually accompanies a bull market.

But a growing economy is a good thing, isn't it? Why would the Fed want to tap on the brakes? Again it comes down to excesses. When the economy is growing too fast, the Fed fears inflation will begin rising, as workers demand higher pay and corporations raise prices to take advantage of the situation. The Fed has always found it difficult to bring inflation back under control once it starts rising. Therefore, it uses interest rates to try to control economic growth to prevent an inflationary spiral from getting started. A hike in interest rates tends to slow the economy, by slowing the willingness of consumers to buy on credit, and increases the cost of corporations to borrow for expansion. That usually cools off the threat of inflation. The downside is that a hike in interest rates also tends to spook the stock market because of that tendency for rate hikes to slow corporate sales and earnings.

However, it's not always rising interest rates that trigger bear markets.

President Kennedy's 1962 speech criticizing U.S. Steel for raising prices was the catalyst for the 1962 bear market. The stock market interpreted the speech to mean the Kennedy administration was going to be hard on business, producing a climate in which corporate earnings would suffer.

The catalyst for the severe 1973–74 bear market has been attributed to the sharp rise in inflation that accompanied the previous bull market.

The Watergate scandal was blamed as the catalyst for the bear market that followed it.

The 1990 bear market was triggered by Iraq's invasion of Kuwait, resulting in crude oil prices surging 100 percent.

The 1981–1982 bear market is thought to have been sparked by a cut in the capital gains tax, which provided a window of opportunity for investors to take their large bull market profits without paying as much out in taxes. Yet, a similar capital gains tax cut in 1997, in an even more overvalued market, had no such effect.

We need to realize that most of the catalysts that analysts believe were the triggers for previous bear markets have been discovered by hindsight. They were not recognized at the time. As the saying goes, "they don't ring a bell at the top." A decline simply begins, worsens into a severe correction, and then further into a bear market. Analysts then look back to determine what the catalyst might have been.

The truth seems to be that once conditions have been set up for a bear market, the market simply uses whatever comes along as an excuse.

THE PROFILE OF A BEAR

It will be of value to look at the profile of a typical bear market.

Since 85 percent of the money currently in the stock market in the late 1990s only began flowing into the market after 1994, the majority of today's investors have never experienced a bear market. For those who have, their most recent experiences were all the way back in 1987 and 1990. Unfortunately, the 1987 and 1990 bear markets were the two shortest bear markets in history, lasting only two or three months. Awareness of their brevity certainly contributes significantly to investors' belief that bear markets are not difficult to hold through.

Normal bear markets have a far different profile.

As mentioned earlier, there have been 29 bear markets over the last 100 years, or 1 on average of every 3 years. They lasted an *average* of fourteen months, but as long as several years. They normally consisted of two or three legs down, interrupted by bear market rallies, and did not end until all excesses had been completely eliminated and stocks had become extremely *under*valued and *under*bought.

The first leg down has typically been the result of some investors, usually beginning with professionals and institutions, already nervous about the overvaluation levels of stocks, noticing some deteriorating condition in surrounding economic conditions. They begin to become concerned about the market's ability to make further gains for a while. At each dip, more are willing to take some profits, deepening the dips, whereas the rallies created when bargain hunters do buy the dips are met by an increasing number of investors willing to immediately sell into the strength each time, causing the rally attempts to fail. The repeated whipsaws cause those who are buying the dips to wait for lower lows each time before being convinced it's time to buy. The resulting bearish pattern of lower lows and lower highs convinces still more participants that the market is topping out, the selling increases, and a significant decline gets underway.

The resulting first leg down works off some of the excesses. Wall Street insists that the sell-off has been overdone, that stocks are a bargain (even though they're still selling at levels of significant overvaluation to their fundamental fair value). A rally begins, and lasts for several months, convincing investors that all is well, and they scramble to become fully invested again.

The second leg down usually begins when it becomes clear that the problems that caused the first leg down, rising inflation or falling earnings, or whatever, were real and not short term. Corporations begin to report declining sales and earnings, or the economic numbers show the economy is slowing dramatically. Since the problems are now more obvious and widely recognized, the second leg down brings in more sellers, so reaches a much lower low before becoming short-term oversold, a condition that is followed by yet another "bear market rally."

The final leg down begins when that rally also fails. When the market rolls over this time, investors begin to panic at the resumption of their losses and the growing gloom and doom in the financial news. This final panic leg down washes out all the previous excesses and interest in speculative investing, and carries valuation levels all the way down into undervalued territory, the exact opposite of the overvaluation levels at the bull market peak. At that point, the buying opportunity of the next ten years is presenting itself.

Unfortunately, by then buy and hold investors, which include the majority of public investors, have bailed out with huge losses and have no interest in the market. Only corporate insiders, institutions, and professionals (who are definitely not buy and hold investors, as we shall see later, tending to sell near the bull market top), have the cash, the interest, and the confidence to load up on the bargains at the bear market low.

So yet another cycle begins.

Whether investors will be made more wealthy or have large losses from participation in the stock market depends not on how large their paper profits are in a bull market, but on how much they give back in the subsequent bear market.

CHAPTER 5

BUY AND HOLD—THE HYPE, THE REALITY

Since in every bull market the vast majority of investors become convinced they should be buy and hold investors, it's necessary to explore that strategy and its chances of success before we even approach the idea of *not* buying and holding, of actually making additional gains rather than giving back, in a bear market.

Obviously, an investor who is committed to a buy and hold approach cannot benefit from markets that are in a downtrend. By definition, they are to hold through all market declines, and then wait until some portion of the next bull market brings their portfolios back up to the levels achieved before the bear market began.

Is a buy and hold strategy a viable approach? Is it perhaps even the best strategy? It's certainly hyped by Wall Street as being so, and in bull markets, when it's easy to adhere to and does outperform other approaches, it certainly becomes *the* market strategy. However, since a bull market is only one side of the cycle, what's the story on buy and hold over the complete cycle, over the long term?

BUY AND HOLD AS A FAILPROOF STRATEGY

Having typically been burned by a previous bear market, having sold out near the bottom and sworn off the "damned market" for good, public investors usually don't become interested in the market again until the next bull market has been underway for quite some time, for most only after it has returned to and exceeded its previous peak. At that time the market's resurrection comes to the attention of the media, the excitement spreads, and public investors soon clamor to get back in.

One of their first insights is that, doggone it, they were wrong to have panicked out in the bear market. They had nice profits in the previous bull market and gave them all up for nothing. The market *did* come back. Now they're buying back in at much higher prices than when they bailed out. Well, that will not happen again. This time they *will* hold through any declines.

Their immediate gains in the new bull market make it seem easy again. Any corrections are again just brief pullbacks, easy to hold through. Brokerage firms, mutual funds, and money management firms get in on the act, pointing out that once again it had been proved how important it is for investors to adopt a long-term outlook, a buy and hold strategy, because the market *always* comes back.

Once again, it becomes an easy sell. Simply buy good stocks or mutual funds, and hold them long term.

And the sales pitch is true, *as it's stated*. The stock market, as measured by the major indexes, although it periodically suffers gut-wrenching declines, *always* comes back from those declines and moves on to even higher highs. You have only to look at the following chart for irrefutable proof.

This chart depicts the Dow Jones Industrial Average (DJIA) from 1915 to 1999. There were, as pointed out in Chapter 1, twenty-nine market declines, plunges, and crashes during the period, with declines as large as 86 percent, and averaging more than 31 percent. Yet the market came back

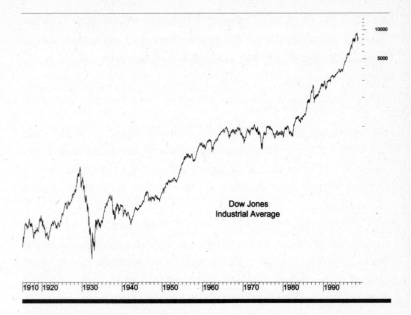

Dow Jones
Industrial Average

from every one of them, even the 1929 crash, and moved on to still higher highs.

Obviously, an investor who simply bought *at any time* through the period and held on long enough, would have had a foolproof system for eventually making long-term gains.

The strategy seems to be devoid of pitfalls. For instance, even if an investor had the bad luck to invest precisely at any of the market peaks, then held on for thirty years, he or she would still have wound up with nice gains.

Need more proof?

Ten thousand dollars invested in a typical growth-oriented mutual fund in 1977, and held through all subsequent market declines over just the next twenty years, would have grown to $210,560 by the end of 1997, a 16 percent annual rate of return.

The statistical glories of buy and hold investing seem to be endless, and provide wonderful sales tools for the "sell side" of Wall Street—brokerage firms, mutual funds, and money managers—who make their income and profits by selling stocks and mutual funds to the public, or through fees charged for managing investors' assets. They can tell investors that there's no need for them to be concerned about risk, or bear markets. There's no need to wait for better market or economic conditions. Just invest anytime, and let time take care of it.

IT MAKES SENSE

Investors are neither dumb nor foolish. They come by their intentions to be determined buy and hold investors each time, based on criteria that any intelligent, thinking person should employ—their own experience, the advice of experts, and a study of history.

Their experience is that it was a mistake to have exited during the previous bear market because the market did come back. That experience is confirmed by experiences in the new bull market, where holding through the brief pullbacks has been the smart strategy since the market has also come back from those each time.

The advice of the experts? Brokerage firms, mutual funds, and money managers go to great lengths to make sure all investors hear the word that they should simply buy and hold, and ignore all market gyrations as just temporary potholes on the road to riches.

Lastly, history certainly proves that the market always comes back. Guarantees it.

So public investors, who just a few years previously, at a bear market low, wanted nothing more to do with the stock market, move once again to the opposite extreme and determine that this time they'll put everything they can raise into the market and will not sell, no matter what.

Comments in "man in the street" TV interviews during brief market declines in 1998 demonstrate the determination that prevails in all bull markets:

> Said one investor, "I'll never sell another stock when it starts to go down. Every time in the past that I did, I looked a few months later and it was back up."

Said another, "Worried? Why would I be worried? The market has its ups and downs, but they are no problem as long as one has a long-term perspective."

An investor whose portfolio was already underwater, was asked if she would lighten up on her holdings. She replied, "Why would anyone with half a brain sell at a loss?"

KEEPING IT REAL

And yet, and yet. Identical evidence, advice, and confident intentions were in place at the top of every bull market in history, *yet no such creature as a buy and hold investor ever emerged from the other side of the subsequent bear market.*

Buy and hold investing, for all its hype, and in spite of the apparent guarantee that history provides for the theory, just does not work. During the euphoria of a bull market, it seems to be easy to picture oneself holding through a bear market, eagerly watching for it to end so the big gains will resume.

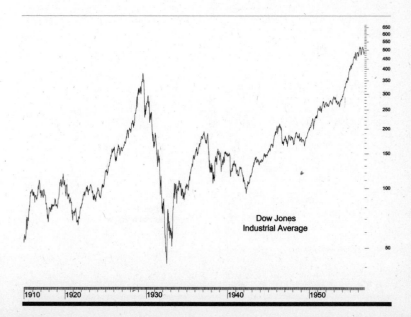

Dow Jones
Industrial Average

However, comes the reality, the emotional and financial pain of watching hard earned assets disappearing 20, 30 percent at a whack, the decline lasting for months, even years, and thoroughly disillusioned, buy and hold investors eventually give up. Unfortunately, they do so with the worst of timing, maximizing losses by selling at or near the bear market low.

The proof is easy enough to find.

There were certainly few investors at all, let alone buy and hold investors, in the aftermath of the 1929 stock market crash, in which the market lost 86 percent of its value, plunging the world into the Great Depression. It took twenty-six years, until 1955, for the market to come back.

There were few buy and hold investors left in 1982, after experiencing a sixteen-year period that began in 1966 (shown in the following chart), during which there were five devastating bear markets of up to 45 percent, while in spite of the subsequent rallies, the market in 1982 was still below its 1966 peak. Sixteen years of whipsawing heartbreak for buy and hold investors.

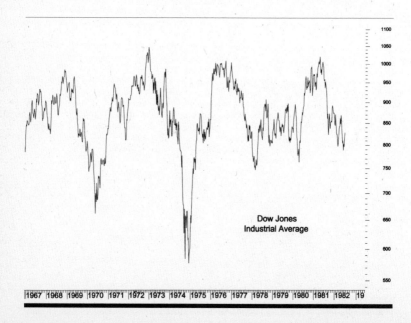

Dow Jones
Industrial Average

How many were still holding after the 1987 crash (pictured here), even though the next bull market began almost immediately?

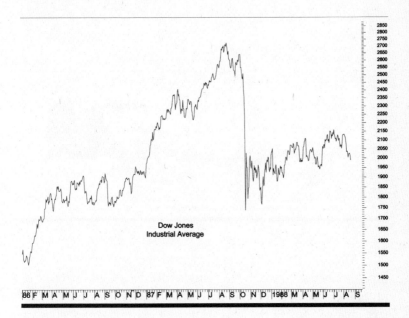

The chart on page 36, courtesy of Ned Davis Research Inc., provides quite clear answers and should be studied closely.

The upper window of the chart shows the Dow Jones Industrial Average from 1960 through late-1998. The lower window of the chart shows the flow of money into and out of mutual funds during the same period. When the graph is below 0, it shows the degree to which investors were pulling money out of mutual funds, and when it's above the 0 line, it shows the level of money flowing into mutual funds.

Note how *after* each bear market (shown in the upper window of the chart) had given them serious losses, investors finally gave up and began withdrawing their money, indicated by the previous inflow reversing to outflow. In several instances, the outflow continued well into and beyond the next bull market.

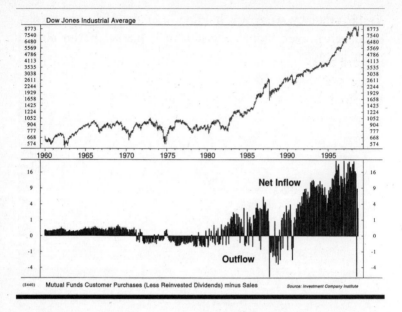

Dow Jones Industrial Average

Mutual Funds Customer Purchases (Less Reinvested Dividends) minus Sales   Source: Investment Company Institute

After the 1982 bear market low, the next generation of investors began to reach their productive years, and interest in investing and mutual funds grew significantly. But did the pattern change? Not in the least. Note that each market decline of more than 10 percent resulted in previous money inflow reversing to outflow, *after* the correction had taken place. The most pronounced reversal to outflow took place after the 1987 market crash. That outflow continued into 1989 even though the next bull market was well underway.

As the revitalized bull market moved higher in 1989 and 1990, money again flowed in. However, came the 1990 bear market, which lasted only three months, and again investors bailed out.

History through the century, through the last bear market in 1990, quite clearly shows that buy and hold investors have always been unable to carry out the second half of their intended strategy, and wound up bailing out at the bear market lows, suffering large losses.

THIS TIME IS DIFFERENT?

Since that last bear market in 1990, the market has hardly experienced even a serious correction, let alone a bear market, the longest such period in history. Not surprisingly, investors have therefore had no trouble buying and holding, and in their growing confidence, have poured money into the stock market as never before, as the chart on page 36 also shows.

That unprecedented inflow of new money created the biggest three-year market rise in history, in 1995, 1996, and 1997, boosting investor confidence in buy and hold investing even higher.

But are 1990's investors so different from their forebears? Will they still be holding after the next bear market has devastated *their* portfolios? Will they patiently, even impatiently, wait, with their portfolios underwater, until the market comes back (as it undoubtedly will)? It doesn't seem so. As the chart shows, investors even began to bail out after the relatively minor 1998 correction.

Let's see if we can find more clues to their staying power. It's very important that we do.

For buy and hold investors, if they are going to bail out of the strategy again this time, they'd be far better off realizing it ahead of time while it can do them some good.

For the rest of us, who already know we would not be able to carry out the second half of a buy and hold strategy, determining whether buy and hold investors will again bail out in the next bear market is also extremely important. Just look at the huge overhang of money that has poured into mutual funds in this bull market as shown in the chart on page 36. If all that money heads for the exit, the selling pressure will be humongous and could turn what might be a normal bear market into a disaster.

So, it's important that we determine what those current investors who view themselves as buy and hold investors will really do when the next bear comes growling.

Where can we find clues? Let's look at markets that have already been mauled by bear markets in the last ten years. How did buy and hold investors of the 1990s react in those?

Investors in the Japanese market in 1989, including U.S. investors, certainly did not continue to hold those investments after the bottom fell out. Their selling exacerbated the decline, with the Japanese market remaining underwater by 65 percent nine years later. In fairness, it was certainly made difficult for them to hold on, given that even the most stalwart of the previous Wall Street bulls on the region quickly gave up at the lows when talk of a prolonged recession in Japan began to prove out. Their advice became on the order of, "I wouldn't venture into Japanese investments quite yet, the recovery may be some years away." For buy and hold investors who were still in, the experts were now saying they shouldn't have been.

How many U.S. investors who piled so heavily into Asian mutual funds in 1995 and 1996, on the promise that the bull market in those tiger economies would last well into the next century, are still confidently holding those investments, waiting for them to come back?

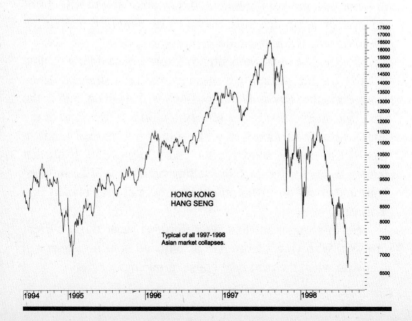

HONG KONG
HANG SENG

Typical of all 1997-1998
Asian market collapses.

We don't have to guess. The following table shows the amount of investor assets that typical Asian/Pacific mutual funds had under management as 1997 began, before the market collapses in the region took place, and how much they were still managing at the end of the year, after the bear markets had taken their toll.

FUND	ASSETS UNDER MANAGEMENT 12/31/96	ASSETS UNDER MANAGEMENT 12/31/97
Fidelity Japanese Small Co. Fund	$291 million	$99 million
Invesco Pacific Basin Fund	$153 million	$53 million
Prudential Pacific Basin Fund	$89 million	$28.5 million
Strong Asia Pacific Fund	$70.4 million	$24.7 million
Merrill Lynch Dragon Fund	$1157 million	$375 million
Morgan Stanley Asia Growth Fund	$209 million	$69.1 million
T. Rowe Price New Asia Fund	$2181 million	$783 million
Scudder Pacific Opportunities Fund	$344 million	$127 million
First Philippine Fund	$225 million	$105 million
Indonesia Fund	$49.2 million	$16.5 million
Korea Fund	$509 million	$221 million
Malaysia Fund	$242 million	$50 million
Thai Fund	$214 million	$46 million
Singapore Fund	$121 million	$66 million

Keep in mind that even a good portion of the assets still under management at the end of 1997 was probably new money that came in *after* the market plunges, buying in on the hope that the next bull market was about to begin.

It's intriguing that many of the same investors who bailed out of their Japanese investments after 1989, and out of Asian markets in 1997 and 1998, are those who believe they will be able to hold through the next bear market in the United States.

WHAT HAPPENS TO BUY AND HOLDERS' DETERMINATION?

Why do they give up at the lows, after sticking with their plan through most of the painful downturn? Primarily because the extreme emotional stress of watching a good portion of their assets disappear eventually becomes unendurable when it becomes obvious that no one knows when it will end. The reality becomes unbearably different from what they imagined during the good times of the previous bull market, when holding through all declines seemed as though it would be a confident period of simply waiting a while for the market to bounce back and the big gains to resume. Part of that imagined scenario also assumed they'd continue to have the support of a confident Wall Street, and a positive media, while hanging on.

So, they start out determined to hold through any decline, perhaps even feeling a bit superior for their calm acceptance of the downturn in the face of the concerns of their friends and associates. However, the average bear market lasts fourteen months, and as we've seen, the problems *can* persist for years. After three months, six months, a year of such erosion, of the emotional stress, of the news getting gloomier, almost all give up on the strategy and bail out.

They discover that it's one thing for a Warren Buffett, Peter Lynch, or John Templeton to hold through bear markets, and advise others to do so. The paper losses do not affect their life in the slightest degree. It's quite another experience for investors who are watching their life savings, or their children's college money, disappear. It's certainly not the same thing for those nearing, or in their retirement years, to see 30, 40, 50 percent of their retirement funds disappear. It's more pain and strain and uncertainty than the soul can stand, some of which can be mercifully ended by simply bailing out and taking the loss. And so they do.

They also feel betrayed when they discover their original reasoning, which seemed so well founded during the bull market—on their own experience, the advice of experts, and the lessons of history—was actually based on a foundation of shifting sands.

First, their experience changes, when what is expected to be just another 10 percent pullback becomes a 20 percent decline, then 30, 40, even 50 percent.

Next, the advice they received from the experts begins to look questionable. As a bear market begins to unfold, Wall Street tells investors to just hang in there. This may be a bit worse than the 10 percent pullbacks they've experienced, but there's no reason to believe the bull market has ended. As the decline slides past 20 percent, the word from Wall Street is that the decline is almost over. That advice, and temporary market bounces, keep buy and hold investors holding on, but increasingly concerned. However, as the downside resumes and the decline exceeds 25 and 30 percent, the previously bullish advisors begin to waffle in their advice, acknowledge that a bear market is underway, and waffle on how long it might be before it ends.

In the meantime, a change takes place in the ranks of experts who are handing out advice. Market timers who had warned a top was approaching, and similar advisors with risk management strategies, who were in disfavor with the media during the euphoric final stages of the bull market, suddenly become the media stars. They were right after all, and so become the experts to whom the media now look for guidance. The financial press resurrects phrases not used since the last bear market: "no bottom in sight," "cash is king," "short sellers are cleaning up."

The guests now being trotted in front of cameras and microphones, and featured in the press, are the short sellers and market timers, those who are making a killing in the bear market. Their advice, of course, is that investors should have bailed out before the bear market got underway, should have moved to the "short" side.

EVEN HISTORY TAKES A TRAITOROUS TURN

It sinks in that a long-term chart is just that. Yes, the market has always come back, but not necessarily in an investor's lifetime.

After the 1929 crash, it took twenty-six years, until 1955, for the Dow to get back to its levels of 1929, and for most of those twenty-six years, it was underwater by 50 to 75 percent. An investor who was forty-five years old in 1929 and somehow did actually hold, would have waited until he or she was seventy-one years old for the market to "come back" to its 1929 level.

And as a previous chart shows, after the market topped out in 1966, it took sixteen years, until 1982, for it to come back to its level of 1966.

Those two periods amounted to forty-two out of the fifty-three years from 1929 to 1982 when buy and hold investors, if there really were such an animal, would have been waiting for the market to come back. No one could be expected to have that much patience, or tolerance for pain, particularly when other investments—real estate, gold, and so on—were soaring and attracting excited attention during much of the period.

EVEN THE THEORY ITSELF IS FLAWED AND DECEPTIVE

Although statistics show that the market always comes back, it's not the *same* market that comes back.

The theory is based on the fact that the thirty-stock Dow Jones Industrial Average, and the S&P 500, always eventually come back from bear markets and go on to new highs. However, the composition of those indexes undergoes such frequent revision as to render that fact meaningless, deceptively misleading.

For example, 30 percent of the stocks that composed the Dow just eleven years ago are no longer part of the Dow now. They were replaced, a few at a time, by stocks of newer, stronger companies that became more representative of the changing economy. It's been the same since the turn of the century. Whole new industries, first railroads and banks, oil exploration firms, and insurance companies, came into being and made up the indexes. I hope no one is still waiting for Distilling & Cattle Feeding Inc. to come back. It was once a Dow stock, as were American Cotton Oil Corp. and U.S. Leather. How about American Locomotive Inc. or Baldwin Locomotive—replaced by the stocks of automobile, drug, and beverage companies. Then it was airlines, aircraft manufacturers, photography, and other newer industries spawning an endlessly changing list of new and exciting companies. The strongest stocks among them periodically displaced fading companies in the Dow and S&P 500.

Many of those exciting industries faded in turn and were replaced by still newer industries: biotechnology, aerospace, nuclear. Exciting stocks of companies that didn't even exist in the prior bull market constantly move into the indexes, displacing faded winners. The 1980's computer wave produced stocks like IBM, Amdahl, Control Data, Adobe Systems, Hewlett Packard, Apple Computer, and Sun Microsystems. Some have already been replaced in the indexes by the 1990's wave of computer-related companies: Dell, Gateway, Intel, Compaq, Microsoft, Seagate, 3Com. Superstores became a major industry, and Circuit City, Home Depot, WalMart, Toys R US, and similar fast-growing stocks from that industry bumped still more faded stocks from the indexes. Clothing stocks became important, and Nike, The Limited, Gap Stores, and Reebok moved into the indexes. Entertainment became a big new industry, and Brunswick, Disney, Calloway Golf, MGM, and Hilton Hotels bumped more fading stocks out of the indexes.

The point is, what does it really mean to say the market always comes back if the indexes that supposedly prove that fact are constantly altered to include only the stocks that are the strongest at the time, while many of the stocks that investors were invested in during the previous bull market, which they really need to come back, have been dropped from the record, and in some cases no longer even exist?

Who knows what exciting new industries will bump current popular stocks from their pedestals? How many new companies that currently exist only in the imaginations of a couple of guys working in *their* parents' garages will fuel the next bull market? Which currently strong stocks won't make the next cut, or the one thereafter? Which are already on their way out to make room for the Internet stocks?

CONCLUSION

Those who advocate a buy and hold strategy for investors in the latter stages of bull markets play a very dirty trick on them.

Not only is the theory itself, that the market always comes back, deceptive if not entirely bogus, but, as in diets, exercise programs, or any human endeavor that requires unusual discipline, it's far more beneficial to advocate a program that can be followed than one that sounds great in theory, and has even worked for specific unusual individuals, but can't be followed to a successful conclusion by anyone else. Current buy and hold investors will discover yet again that it's a strategy that just can't be followed when the devastation hits.

Furthermore, even if one *could* stick with a buy and hold strategy through all bear markets, and even if when the market comes back an investor could know that his or her stocks would also come back, studies show that buy and hold does not compare profitwise or riskwise with even a small degree of success in just standing aside for a portion of downturns, and then re-entering at lower prices to make some of the gains over again.

CHAPTER 6

RIDE BOTH BULL AND BEAR MARKETS

We probably all agree that it's not too difficult to make gains in a bull market. After all, a rising market carries most stocks up with it.

However, the degree to which those gains can be maximized, *while risk is actually reduced*, may surprise you. In addition, the same system that allows you to maximize gains in a bull market will provide the cash to make *further gains* from bear markets (instead of waiting with increasing losses for the market to come back).

The first way to profit from a bear market is obviously not to allow it to take back too much of the gains made in the previous bull market. Any degree of success at all in exiting before, or shortly after, a bear market begins produces startling results. Not only are the profits already made in the bull market kept, but one is then able to buy back in at lower prices and make at least some of the gains over again.

Many investors don't realize, even if they could be successful in holding through a bear market, how much of the next bull market they'd need just to get their portfolios back to even. For instance, picture an investor with a portfolio worth $100,000. A bear market comes along that takes that portfolio down 40 percent to $60,000. That investor will then need, not a 40 percent gain, but a 66 percent gain, to get back to where he or she was at $100,000. If the investor's portfolio declines

50 percent to $50,000, he or she will need a 100 percent gain to get it back to even. Not easy things to come by, even 66 percent gains. For instance, although one of the best three-year periods the market has ever enjoyed, from 1995 through 1997, produced gains in the S&P 500 of 34, 20, and 31 percent, in the preceding period from 1991 through 1994, the S&P 500 gained only 28 percent *for the entire four-year period*. Yet, the same bull market was underway, and there were no bear markets or serious corrections during the interval. Allowing a portfolio to lose 40 percent, then needing gains of 66 percent just to get back to even, obviously puts an investor in a difficult position.

However, investors who are successful *to any degree* in taking their profits, even after a bear market has been underway for a while, and then buy back in at lower prices, will have significantly better results, and just as important, will not suffer the financial and emotional strain of having their portfolio down 40 or 50 percent for perhaps a long period.

Some years ago, Norman Fosback, of the Institute for Econometric Research, in Deerfield Beach, Florida, performed a study of alternative market strategies, covering the period from 1964 to 1984. Using the S&P 500 as a proxy for the market, he found that starting with $100,000, a buy and hold strategy produced $775,000 of profit for the period.

However, if an investor could have timed every 5 percent and larger swing of the market, and profited on both the upside and the downside, just $10,000 would have grown to $5.2 *billion* in the same period. Of course, that's a ridiculous comparison, which Fosback included in the study only to make a point. No one can time all, or even most, of the 5 percent swings in the market (roughly 450 points on the Dow at 1999 levels), particularly over a period of twenty years. But unless your name is Trump, do you really need $5.2 billion to feel comfortable?

Well then, Fosback's study showed that if an investor could have timed only the *major* swings, he or she still would have turned $100,000 into $13,810,000!

Still too difficult?

Okay. Timing the market just successfully enough to avoid only the three worst downturns that occurred during the twenty years would still have turned $100,000 into $4,797,000, almost six times as much as a buy and hold strategy.

In fact, Fosback found that any degree of success at all in avoiding even a portion of the downdrafts has a tremendous effect on long-term accumulation of wealth. His study showed that if one recognized bear markets only perceptively enough to sell short for one-fourth of each of the three worst corrections during the twenty-year period, *and remained invested all the rest of the time*, he or she still would have tripled the return of the much vaunted buy and hold strategy.

You'll never hear that from Wall Street, however, where the advice, at least for public investors, is that "market timing doesn't work," that "no one can time the market," that investors should simply buy and hold. Unfortunately, the securities industry takes considerable liberty with the facts in attempting to prove that self-serving premise to investors.

For instance, in 1995, Wall Street pounced on a study that showed that if an investor had invested $1000 in the market in 1963 and just left it there, it would have become worth $23,000 by 1993. But if, in an attempt to time the market, the same investor had missed just the ninety best up days during the thirty years, the $1000 would have grown to only $1100. Wall Street claimed the study proves it's too risky to try to time the periods when you should be in the market since you might miss out on too many of the best up days. That information, spread as fact by the media, became a convincing argument that closed many investor's minds to considering market timing as a strategy.

Unfortunately, the rest of the study's findings were not publicized. Those revealed that if, through the same market timing, an investor successfully missed just the ninety *worst* days of the period, the $1000 would have become $320,600. Avoiding at least a portion of market declines is obviously far more beneficial than staying always in harm's way in order to "get" all the market's big up days.

However, more revealing even than what they say or don't say, is the fact that market timing, not buy and hold, is the approach used by those same Wall Street institutions, market professionals, corporate insiders, and large individual investors, for their *own* money.

BROKERAGE FIRMS

Brokerage firms, trading primarily for their own accounts, utilize market timing almost exclusively. It's hard to believe, but in 1998, their trading in and out of the market through computerized buy and sell programs accounted for more than 20 percent of all the volume on the NYSE. Buy and hold? As even casual observance of daily market activity reveals, some days their "holding" lasts no more than a few hours. If one of their computerized buy programs, in which they buy a huge "basket" of stocks, sparks an intraday rally, and the market spurts up 1, 2 percent, they almost instantly institute massive sell programs to take their quick profits. Their activity so overwhelms the market at times that, in 1987, the SEC mandated trading curbs that limit such computerized trades when they roil the market too violently intraday. Surprisingly, according to annual reports of the SEC, brokerage firms earn more from such trading in their own accounts than they do from commission and fee income.

They may tell investors to simply buy and hold, but isn't it interesting that brokerage firms rarely risk such a strategy for their own money, even overnight. Their frenetic market timing works well for them, too. In 1994, the last year the S&P 500 was down for the year on a buy and hold basis, brokerage firms still earned a whopping $20.2 billion from such short-term timing, almost unchanged from the previous year.

MUTUAL FUNDS

Mutual fund managers are the so-called long-term end of the market. Surely, they practice the buy and hold strategy they pitch to public investors.

No. Again it's a case of do as I say, not as I do. A perusal of the Morningstar database of mutual funds shows hundreds of funds have annual portfolio turnover rates of 100 to 300 percent, even more. Yes, a 100 percent turnover rate means turning over their entire portfolio on average of every twelve months; a 300 percent turnover rate indicates an average holding period of just four months. The following table shows the portfolio turnover rates for some of the larger, more popular funds.

FUND	1993	1994	1995	1996	1997
		ANNUAL PORTFOLIO TURNOVER RATE			
AIM WEINGARTEN A	109%	136%	139%	159%	—
AARP CAPITAL GROWTH	101%	80%	98%	65%	39%
THE JANUS FUND	127%	139%	118%	104%	132%
BERGER 100 FUND	74%	64%	114%	122%	200%
TEMPLETON GLOBAL INCOME	265%	138%	104%	113%	192%
INVESCO DYNAMICS	144%	169%	175%	196%	204%
THE DREYFUS FUND	39%	28%	269%	221%	201%
FIDELITY MAGELLAN	155%	132%	120%	155%	67%
PHOENIX BALANCED A	130%	159%	197%	191%	206%
KEMPER TOTAL RETURN	180%	121%	142%	85%	122%
SMITH BARNEY MNGD MUNIS	206%	131%	100%	80%	103%
CGM CAPITAL DEVELOPMENT	143%	146%	271%	178%	—
STRONG TOTAL RETURN	271%	290%	—	502%	—

You'll recognize a number of them as being managed or owned by charismatic spokespeople who travel the financial talk show circuit, telling investors the only way to make money in the market is to buy and hold good stocks long term, and totally avoid efforts to time the market. That's not the way they handle the investments in their funds.

It's interesting that when Peter Lynch, the most successful mutual fund manager of all time, was managing Fidelity's Magellan fund, considered to have been the best-performing mutual fund of all time, he turned its portfolio over 300 percent per year, an average holding period of just four months for each stock in its huge portfolio. Since his retirement from fund management in 1988, and appointment as Fidelity's chief public spokesperson, his advice to investors has been to simply buy good stocks or mutual funds and put them away for the very long term, making no attempt to time their ups and downs.

CORPORATE INSIDERS

How about corporate insiders, the managers and largest stockholders of corporations? We know they don't want *you* trading in and out of their stocks, but how do they handle *their* holdings in the same stocks?

They can't hide their activity. SEC rules require insiders to file all changes in their stock holdings in a timely manner. Month after month, year after year, those filings clearly show how persistently and successfully company insiders trade in and out of their company's stock, sometimes several times a year, selling after prices have rallied, buying back after the stock has declined back to lower levels. Corporate insiders are so successful with their market timing that Wall Street professionals and astute investors use measurements of which companies have insiders buying and which have insiders selling as important research to guide their own investments.

Information on buying or selling activity by corporate insiders is of such importance, and in such demand, that a number of firms are in business solely to collect, analyze, and sell the information.

By the way, lest there be any misunderstanding, we are talking about legal insider trading. Corporate insiders are allowed to trade in and out of their company's stock to their heart's content, as long as they don't make such trades based on information that is not available to the public, and as long as they report the changes in their holdings to the SEC. Illegal insider trading consists of trading on "secret" information that has not yet been made public.

BIG-NAME INVESTORS

Joseph P. Kennedy, Bernard Baruch, Jesse Livermore, J. P. Morgan, John D. Rockefeller, and many more, from a previous era, George Soros, Paul Tudor Jones, Jimmy Rogers, the Bass Brothers, Julian Robertson, Richard Rainwater, Michael Steinhardt, and many more, from the present era, were market timers all. Either they buy stocks, currencies, bonds, commodities, and gold when prices are depressed and sell them as soon as they're high, or they sell them short when prices are high and buy them back after they decline.

Try to compile a similar list of successful buy and hold investors. In fact, the next time someone tells you the only way to invest is to buy and hold, challenge him or her to name *anyone* who has become an outstanding investor by holding a portfolio for *any* twenty-year period ever. The first, and perhaps only name out of his or her mouth will be Warren Buffett, but just say, sorry, Warren belongs in the list of market timers. Just look at the facts.

Buffett has carefully nurtured his image of being just a simple investor in Omaha, who started out picking stocks based on whether the company was "one I'd like to own even if there were no stock market," and by just holding those stocks forever became a multibillionaire. The facts are quite different.

Far from being a simple investor whom anyone can emulate, Buffett grew up in the securities business. His father owned a brokerage firm in Omaha. Warren made his first millions running private investment partnerships for wealthy investors. After making them huge gains in the mid-1960's bull market, he demonstrated exquisite market timing at the bull market peak in early 1969 by withdrawing from the market entirely, liquidating the partnerships, and returning most of the assets to the investors.

In the meantime, he began accumulating the depressed shares of Berkshire Hathaway, a rundown textile business, and soon had controlling interest. He sold off its textile operations and turned Berkshire Hathaway into a holding company for investments, which he started making again once the 1969–70 bear market ended. He began by purchasing small private companies like See's Candy. Over the years, those companies came to also include Nebraska Furniture Mart, Borshein's Jewelry, and World Book Encyclopedias. In 1976, he gained control of financially troubled Geico Insurance. Berkshire Hathaway has never parted with those private companies, or Geico Insurance, all of which were bought with the intention of operating them as subsidiaries, giving rise to the myth that Buffett buys and holds *all* investments for the long term.

However, that's not close to true. When it comes to Berkshire Hathaway's investments in publicly traded stocks, those stocks that the public flocks into as soon as they learn that Buffett has taken a large position, those stocks whose value fluctuates up and down, virtually none have remained in its portfolio from one bull market to the next. Even *during* bull markets, Buffett doesn't hesitate to buy and sell such holdings. Normally involved with very large positions in only seven or eight companies at a time, and secretive about his holdings, Buffett just over the last few years, appears to have traded in and out of large positions in Salomon Bros., U.S. Air Group, McDonald's, zero coupon bonds, and silver. He also apparently dumped significant holdings when the market began topping out in July 1998 since, by September, Berkshire Hathaway was holding a huge $9 billion in cash.

Whether he admits it or not, Warren Buffett is the epitome of a market timer. By being such, he has become one of the wealthiest people in the world and made many stockholders of Berkshire Hathaway very wealthy as well. I'm not sure the same can be said of investors who try to ride on his coattails by buying stocks after they learn Buffett has taken large positions. Frequently, the news is not made public until many months after he has the positions. By then, the stock has usually had a nice rise, leaving public investors buying "high." At the other end of the situation, when those stocks eventually hit the downside of their cycle, investors may well find out far too late that exquisite timer Buffett disposed of his positions at the highs.

It's also interesting that Warren Buffett is a self-proclaimed disciple of his former mentor, Benjamin Graham, and Graham's rule for holding stocks was, "Sell after holding for two years, or after the stock has risen 50 percent, whichever comes first."

NOT A NEW PHENOMENON

The situation of big-name investors being market timers is also not a new phenomenon. Name any old-time, well-known family fortune made in the stock market, and you can know it was achieved by a market timer, trading in and out of individual stocks as market leadership changed in bull markets, selling short in bear markets, trading in and out of stocks in which they were corporate insiders. Joseph P. Kennedy, Bernard Baruch, J. P. Morgan, John D. Rockefeller, Pulitzer, Carnegie. No wipeout in the 1929 stock market crash for them.

KEEP AN OPEN MIND

All this is by means of convincing you to approach the thought of market timing with an open mind, unhampered by the self-serving propaganda of Wall Street. Realize that market timing does work very well, indeed, and is, and always has been, utilized by the majority of professional investors, institutions, and insiders, the very same who advocate a buy and hold strategy for public investors, the very same who claim that market timing does not work.

Not only does it work, but it's nowhere nearly as difficult to accomplish as Wall Street would have you believe.

MARKET TIMING WITH TECHNICAL INDICATORS

We provide the following chart just to whet your appetite for now.

The upper graph in the chart shows a technical momentum indicator, known as the MACD trigger. Its formula and use are

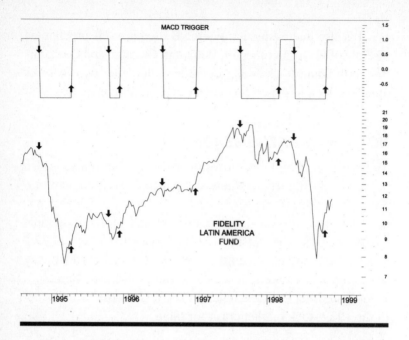

detailed later. We show it only as an example of the types of tools that are used for market timing. This particular indicator compiles daily or weekly changes in upside and downside momentum. Applied to a stock, mutual fund, or the overall market, it triggers buy and sell signals when the changes become significant enough to indicate a trend has reversed. The lower graph in the chart shows daily closes of the Fidelity Latin America mutual fund in relation to those buy and sell signals.

As shown, over the period from 1994 to 1998, the MACD trigger produced a buy signal an average of once a year, as indicated by the up arrows on the graph. If an investor entered the fund at the buy signal and held until the indicator triggered a sell signal, and repeated the process, he or she would have participated in most of each rally, and avoided most of each decline, making gains over and over, significantly beating a buy and hold strategy. Typically, a buy and hold investor in the fund would have made temporary gains but then given them back, winding up going nowhere. The following table shows the comparison.

TRADE SIGNAL	DATE	FUND PRICE	GAIN OR LOSS
Buy	7/29/94	$12.69	
Sell	11/11/9	$15.54	+12.6%
Buy	4/21/95	$9.18	
Sell	10/27/9	$9.26	+1%
Buy	12/22/9	$10.05	
Sell	7/26/96	$11.88	+16.9%
Buy	1/10/97	$13.64	
Sell	8/22/97	$18.03	+32%
Buy	3/6/98	$16.61	
Sell	5/22/98	$15.25	-8%

Compounded total gain over the five trades = **+69.1%**

Gain from buy and hold 7/29/94 to 5/22/98 = **+10.5%**

The gain from buying and selling with the MACD trigger indicator was more than *six times* as much as the gain an investor would have had by buying the fund on 7/29/94 and holding through the ups and downs.

Realize that this is a simplified demonstration provided as an example of the methodology. Although this single indicator worked well on this fund, no one indicator would normally be used in isolation like this.

Later, we'll get into the details of using this simple technical indicator in conjunction with fundamental and seasonal indicators to provide an investment system that, back-tested over thirty-five years, has almost tripled the return of a buy and hold strategy, *and at half the risk*. For now, I just want you to realize that market timing is not, as many seem to think, based on trying to guess what the condition of the economy, or a scandal in

Washington, or IBM's stock split, or Hong Kong's market crash, or the current price-to-earnings ratio, might mean for upcoming market direction.

True market timing is based primarily on *letting the market tell you* when a trend has reversed in a significant way.

MECHANICAL SYSTEMS

Most investors, for whom investing is a sideline, need go no further than uncomplicated mechanical systems that achieve impressive results while making *no* attempt to time the market, no attempt to even recognize bull or bear markets. They're simply predicated on being in the market during periods that have very high odds of the market rising, and safely on the sidelines collecting risk-free interest in CDs or money market accounts at all other times. You'll be amazed at the results such systems achieve at considerably less risk than a buy and hold strategy.

TWO TUMBLES AND A JUMP

One of the first mechanical systems unearthed was the "Two Tumbles and a Jump" indicator discovered by Edson Gould in 1973. Gould discovered that following the dictates of one simple rule would have made investing simple, low risk, and very profitable for the entire fifty-nine year period from 1914 to 1973. The rule is defined as "Two Tumbles Brings a Jump." It's based on the fact that when the Federal Reserve eases its monetary policy, it almost always has a positive effect on the stock market. The Fed eases monetary policy by decreasing one of its three policy variables (the discount rate, margin requirements, or bank reserve requirements). The rule states that when the Fed makes two successive easing moves, a jump in stock prices will follow the second easing. Such a strategy is simple for investors to follow since such changes by the Federal Reserve are always front-page news.

Norman Fosback updated Gould's work on "Two Tumbles Brings a Jump" in 1984, adding an additional decade to the record and showing that during the sixty-nine-year period from 1914 to 1983, if an investor had bought into the market at each of the "Two Tumbles" signals, and simply sold one year later, he or she would have turned $100,000 into $5,423,040 and would have had his or her money at risk in the market for only seventeen of those sixty-nine years and safely earning interest in the bank, or preferably in some other investment than the stock market, during the other fifty-two years.

Note that the investor is not trying to forecast bear markets, or pick market tops, but is simply exiting the market each time, one year after the Federal Reserve signal tells him or her to buy.

Even more revealing, if the investor had instead remained *out* of the market during those seventeen favorable years, and *in* the market the other fifty-two years, his or her $100,000 would have *declined* to $64,500.

Updating the strategy, there was an additional buy signal in 1990, virtually at the 1990 bear market low, and another in 1995, which was followed by the surging market of 1996 and 1997. The most recent buy signal came on October 15, 1998, virtually at the low of the 19 percent July–October correction, when the Federal Reserve cut the Fed funds rate for the second time in three weeks. The Dow surged up 1365 points in six weeks on the news.

However, a strategy that requires waiting for those infrequent "Two Tumbles" signals would probably require too much patience in the current impatient world. Additionally, selling just one year after getting the buy signal, and then frequently watching the market move still higher for perhaps several more years before the inevitable next bear market, would also be a problem for most investors. Most would see they were being left behind, would abandon the strategy, and re-enter the market, frequently just in time to get mauled by the next devastating bear market.

CHAPTER 7

THE BEST MECHANICAL SYSTEM EVER

How would you like a strategy that you can learn in five minutes, that requires virtually no knowledge of how the markets work, requires practically none of your time, yet produces gains that at least equal the highly touted buy and hold strategy on a direct comparison basis, greatly exceeds the performance of a buy and hold strategy on a risk adjusted basis, and avoids almost all the nerve-wracking volatility of the bull market–bear market cycles?

While we're dreaming, let's throw in a few other attributes. How about if this ideal strategy set you free from monitoring the market not only on a daily or weekly basis, but was such that you'd have to look at the market only every six months or so?

What if the only "tools" you need are the information in this chapter, the ability to ignore the hype of Wall Street (which this book should provide you), and a calendar?

What if this system would be welcomed by your broker since it's also to his or her advantage, in that it greatly increases the odds his or her recommendations will make gains for you, at the same time that it's not based on buy and hold but requires that you make commission-producing portfolio changes twice a year?

It's long been said that the best inventions and products evolve from taking a new look at existing processes, using information that's right under our noses to improve on pioneering efforts that have gone before. That's been true of everything from color photography and talking movies to heart surgery and the Internet.

As a brief background, we are in our twelfth year of providing a stock market advisory service to professionals and serious investors. Over the years, we've been consistently ranked in the top-ten market timers in the United States by the rating service *Timer Digest*. However, our work has been primarily based on technical charting and analysis that is not entirely understood by many investors. We realized that investors were in serious need of an advisory service that would tell it like it is regarding the propaganda from Wall Street, *and* have a top market timing system that's as easy to understand as Wall Street's buy and hold advice.

I'll leave out the years of fruitless search for a perfect technical indicator that would eliminate the need for analysis of market internals, investor sentiment, insider activity, seasonality, cycles, and so on. I'll leave out the trips down dead-end rabbit trails checking out the supposed discoveries of others.

SEASONALITY

The breakthrough came when we simply took a new look, via the wonders of computer power, at seasonal stock market tendencies. We already had a handle on technical and fundamental analysis that was putting us in the top-ten ranking of market timers. What if we could combine the simplest of those technical indicators with the most consistent seasonal tendencies to produce a system that would provide above-average results, and yet could be implemented by busy investors, without their having to become full-time market timers?

The results have amazed us, and we believe will amaze you.

Some of the market's "seasonal" tendencies discovered over the years include:

- The four-year presidential cycle
- The first halves of months versus the last halves

- The strong tendency for the seventh and tenth year of each decade to be negative
- The January effect
- January as a barometer for the rest of the year
- September as a reverse barometer for the fourth quarter
- October's tendency to produce downside violence
- The tendency for a "Santa Claus" rally in late December
- The monthly strength period as one month rolls over to the next
- The positive tendency of monthly options expiration weeks
- The positive tendency around holidays

And on and on.

We won't try to give specific credit to those who have pioneered these discoveries since the provenance of some has become cloudy as they have passed into the public domain.

However, Yale Hirsch certainly produced ground-breaking studies of a number of them, and for twenty-eight years has kept track of seasonal tendencies in his annual *Stock Trader's Almanac*.

Norman Fosback of the Institute for Econometric Research produced pioneering work in discovering a number of others.

Among its many types of market research, the esteemed Ned Davis Research Inc. has uncovered still others.

Our goal was to measure the value of each tendency and come up with a seasonal *system,* or trading strategy, that would outperform *and* would be easy to understand and follow. Although many seasonal market tendencies are consistent (or is it persistent) for one reason or another, they turned out to be impractical, or too difficult to incorporate into a usable system. However, two patterns in particular filtered out that appeared to have considerable promise.

It's long been realized that the fall and winter months tend to be considerably more positive for the market than the summer months. We've used that tendency in an undefined manner in our market timing for many years, giving more weight to technical buy signals that occur in the fall and winter, and more weight to technical sell signals that occur in the summer months. However, our use of the information was not formulated, but was more in the form of a "sense of the market" that goes along with good market timing.

In the meantime, Ned Davis Research and Yale Hirsch published research years ago showing December through April periods had better average returns than other times of the year. Their research also showed that the largest stock market declines tended to take place in the spring and early fall.

In 1993, Ned Davis Research Inc. published a promising study comparing the results of being invested in the market from October 1 to May 1 each year to being invested only in the opposite period, the five months from May 1 to October 1.

A number of years ago, Yale Hirsch published research showing that November, December, and January tended to be the most persistently positive months of the year, and a promising study of the results of being invested only for the *six* months between May 1 and November 1 each year, compared to being invested only in the opposite period of November 1 to May 1.

Alan Newman, of *Crosscurrents,* compiled the record from 1950 through April 1997, half a century that included war and peace, boom times and recessions, bull markets and bear markets. His study showed that if an investor, beginning with $100,000 in 1950, had simply adopted a strategy of buying the thirty stocks in the Dow Jones Industrial Average every November 1, and sold out each April 30, holding cash until the following November 1, and then repeated the process year after year, the $100,000 would have become $2,761,113 by April 1997.

However, if an investor adopted the opposite strategy, that is, had been fully invested in the unfavorable May 1 to November 1 periods, and in cash in the favorable November 1 to April 30 periods, the $100,000 would have grown by just $14,840.

Staying in the market year round in order to try to pick up gains in the unfavorable periods obviously added next to nothing to overall portfolio value over the years.

We can update the record to include the last two years:

	Dow Jones Industrial Average
Nov. 1, 1996 to May 1, 1997 (favorable period)	+16.4%
May 1, 1997 to Nov. 1, 1997 (unfavorable period)	+6.2%
Nov. 1, 1997 to May 1, 1998 (favorable period)	+21.8%
May 1, 1998 to Nov. 1, 1998 (unfavorable period)	-6%

So, the seasonal tendencies have continued.

EXPLORING THE REASONS

We refuse to pay attention to statistics, indicators, or systems for which there are no fundamental explanations. So we had to ask, why would the market tend to be very positive for the same six-month period almost every year, and have such a dismal record for the opposite six months?

There seems to be a clear explanation.

Large sums of money are paid to potential investors during the favorable period of November 1 to May 1 each year, much of which finds its way into the stock market. For instance:

- Investors receive Christmas bonuses, year-end bonuses, year-end distributions from profit-sharing plans, and income tax refunds during the period.
- Almost all mutual funds make their major dividend and capital gains distributions in December.
- Private business owners close their books for the prior year in January and February, and once the results are known, distribute the profits to themselves.

- Corporations, once their year-end results are known, pay year-end performance bonuses to management (and make dividend distributions to stockholders).

It certainly makes sense that these events would bring considerable extra buying pressure to the stock market during the same period every year.

Now, is there a similar explanation for why the May 1 to November 1 period would be unfavorable?

It does seem so:

- Beginning in April, those big windfalls dry up, reason enough by itself that the stock market would run out of steam. Remember what happens to the rising river when it runs out of melting snow.
- Worse, investors' cash flow actually heads in the other direction. For those who didn't receive income tax refunds, bank accounts have to be drained, and stocks and mutual funds sold to raise cash, to *pay* income taxes.
- Credit card bills from the heady spending of the Christmas season become a worry and need to be paid down.
- Money is set aside for upcoming summer vacations.
- Investors then take those vacations, paying less attention to the market; the larger the investor the longer and more frequent the vacations.

These explanations made even more sense after we back-tested the statistics and discovered the seasonal differences were not consistent prior to 1947, in the era before significant income taxes, before mutual funds and their year-end distributions, before profit sharing and pension plans, and before the proliferation of small businesses, all of which concentrate the distribution of large chunks of cash in the November to May period.

PLEASE DON'T TELL THE PUBLIC

Wall Street is aware of the seasonal pattern, in general if not in detail, and in fact contributes to it. It's more than just the weather that prompts so many Wall Street professionals to take some chips off the table in May and head out to the Hamptons for the summer. It's a running joke in the media, but an annual event that's clearly measurable by the way the market almost always has a mild correction in the spring (as Wall Streeters lighten up), and then much lighter trading volume through the summer months.

Why doesn't Wall Street push this seasonal pattern that indicates it would produce almost market matching returns, yet with lower market risk? Can you imagine Wall Street's financial problems if investors confined their buying to six months out of the year or left their money in mutual funds only half of the time? Mutual funds in particular would shudder at such a strategy. Once an investor removes his or her assets from a fund, the fund has no assurance whatever that the investor will come back to the same fund later.

No, investors *must* be trained to "buy and hold," trained to "pay no attention to the market's gyrations," trained to "buy the dips," trained to realize that "no one can time the market." *Whoa!* What was that last item? Public investors can't read a calendar accurately enough to know when its May 1, when its November 1?

THE NEXT STEP IN DEVELOPING THE SEASONAL TIMING SYSTEM

The summer–winter seasonal pattern was a big step toward our goal. It came close to matching a buy and hold strategy. It provided a holding period we could easily accept since those using mutual funds would not upset the fund managers with short-term trading. However, our goal was to combine two or more seasonal tendencies, and simple technical indicators, into a trading system that would *beat* a buy and hold strategy.

ADDING A SHORT-TERM SEASONAL TENDENCY

A seasonal tendency we've used for many years is what we call "the monthly strength period." Again, it's not an unknown phenomenon. Yale Hirsch calls it "the monthly bulge." Norman Fosback uses it as a major part of a very short-term trading "seasonality portfolio."

The monthly strength period consists of the last trading day of each month and the first four trading days of the following month. The strength in the market on those five days each month seems to be caused by the fact that high-income investors are usually paid monthly rather than weekly, and institutions operate on monthly fiscal reporting systems.

The result is that over the last fifty years extra money has tended to flow into the market at month ends. The average gains made *in just those five days* have come close to being equal to the average gains made in the other fifteen trading days each month. That's an outstanding ratio.

So our first step toward enhancing the six-month seasonal system was to use entry and exit days that would incorporate the tendencies of the monthly strength period. In theory, if the market's average gain in those five days equals almost half of the average gain for the whole month, we could theoretically pick up the equivalent of a half month of gains *at each end* of each holding period, obtaining seven months of gains on average in each six-month holding period, enough to make a substantial difference when compounded over the long term.

THE RESULTS

So, at this point, the rules for our seasonal system became:

Enter the market the day before the last trading day of October.

Exit on the fourth trading day of the following May.

The table shows the results compounded since 1945, based on the closing price of the Dow Jones Industrial Average on each entry and exit day.

ENTRY YEAR	DJIA AT ENTRY	DJIA AT EXIT	PERCENTAGE GAIN	COMPOUNDED ANNUALLY	BUY AND HOLD COMPOUNDED
1945	184.2	202.5	9.9%	9.93%	9.93%
1946	164.2	174.2	6.1%	16.63%	-5.43%
1947	181.3	180.9	-0.2%	16.37%	-1.79%
1948	188.3	176.3	-6.4%	8.96%	-4.29%
1949	190.4	214.9	12.9%	22.98%	16.67%
1950	226.4	262.8	16.1%	42.75%	42.67%
1951	260.5	261.5	0.4%	43.30%	41.97%
1952	265.7	278.1	4.7%	49.98%	50.98%
1953	276.3	320.4	16%	73.92%	73.94%
1954	354.6	423.4	19.4%	107.7%	129.9%
1955	454.9	516.4	13.5%	135.7%	180.3%
1956	486.5	496.3	2.0%	140.5%	169.4%
1957	435.8	463.7	6.4%	155.9%	151.7%
1958	543.3	624.4	24.9%	194.1%	239%
1959	645.1	608.3	-5.7%	177.3%	230.2%
1960	580.9	692.2	19.2%	230.4%	275.8%
1961	701.1	671.2	-4.2%	216.4%	264.4%
1962	589	713.8	21.2%	283.4%	287.5%
1963	755.2	828.2	9.7%	320.4%	349.6%
1964	871.9	933.5	7.1%	350.1%	406.8%
1965	959.1	900	-6.2%	322.4%	388.6%
1966	808	901.9	11.6%	371.5%	389.6%
1967	886.6	914.5	3.2%	386.3%	396.5%
1968	951.1	962.1	1.12%	391.9%	422.3%
1969	850.5	718.4	-15.5%	315.5%	290.%
1970	753.6	937.4	24.4%	416.9%	408.9%
1971	837.6	937.3	11.9%	478.4%	408.8%
1972	946.4	953.9	0.8%	483.0%	417.9%
1973	968.5	844.9	-12.8%	408.6%	358.7%
1974	673	834.7	24.0%	530.8%	353.2%

ENTRY YEAR	DJIA AT ENTRY	DJIA AT EXIT	PERCENTAGE GAIN	COMPOUNDED ANNUALLY	BUY AND HOLD COMPOUNDED
1975	839.4	989.5	17.9%	643.6%	437.2%
1976	952.6	943.4	-1.0%	636.4%	412.2%
1977	822.7	824.4	0.2%	637.9%	347.6%
1978	791.4	847.5	7.1%	690.2%	360.1%
1979	823.8	816	-0.9%	682.8%	343.%
1980	917.8	973.3	6.15%	730.1%	428.4%
1981	832.9	863.2	3.6%	760.3%	368.6%
1982	991	1219.7	23.1%	958.8%	562.2%
1983	1233.5	1165	-5.5%	900.0%	532.5%
1984	1217.3	1247.8	2.5%	925.1%	577.4%
1985	1375.6	1787.9	30%	1232%	870.6%
1986	1878.4	2342.2	24.79%	1561%	1171.5%
1987	1938.3	2020.2	4.2%	1631%	996.7%
1988	2149.9	2384.9	10.9%	1820%	1195%
1989	2603.5	2710.4	4.1%	1899%	1371%
1990	2448	2941.6	20.2%	2302%	1497%
1991	3071.8	3369.4	9.7%	2535%	1729%
1992	3246.3	3441.9	6.0%	2694%	1769%
1993	3687.9	3696	0.2%	2700%	1906%
1994	3930.7	4360	10.9%	3006%	2267%
1995	4756.6	5464	14.9%	3468%	2866%
1996	5993.2	7225.3	20.6%	4202%	3822%
1997	7381.7	9054.7	22.7%	**5177%**	**4816%**

Not bad. Over a fifty-year period, our enhanced seasonal system beat the market's points gain, therefore a buy and hold strategy, by a ratio of 5,177 to 4,816 percent. In terms of dollars, if we had started out with $100,000 the seasonal system would have wound up with $5,177,000. The buy and hold strategy would have wound up with $4,816,000.

Just as important, using the seasonal system, our money would have been at risk only six months out of every twelve. *So, the system beat the market and a buy and hold strategy, with just half the risk.*

However, we're teasing you. This was just the preliminary test to determine whether holding only in the favorable seasonal period would actually beat the market's return for the full year, on a bare bones comparison of the market's price moves during the periods.

We didn't include dividends, or the fact that the buy and hold investor would have been in the market twice as long each year, so would have collected twice as much in dividends. As Wall Street correctly points out, dividends account for a good portion of the market's "total return" over the long term.

However, on the other side of the ledger, we didn't include the fact that while the buy and hold investor was collecting six months of extra dividends, the follower of the seasonal system would have been receiving interest on cash in the bank for those six months.

Now we'll run a study that credits the market on a buy and hold basis with the dividends paid by the Dow's stocks each year. For the seasonal system, we'll include only half the annual dividends, since paid quarterly, it will receive only half the year's total. However, we'll also credit the follower of the seasonal system with six months of interest on cash when out of the market. We'll assume he or she put the cash into short-term T bills at their market exit each year since it's easier to come up with accurate figures for T bills going back several decades than it is to come up with average figures on what banks were paying for interest rates. Yes, that does throw the numbers off in favor of the buy and hold strategy by a considerable margin since interest rates on CDs and money market accounts are higher than the yield on T bills. But that's okay. We'll give the buy and hold strategy that advantage in the study. We already know how it's going to come out because even T bill yields are usually higher than stock dividends.

The following table goes back thirty-five years, comparing the total return of our new Seasonal Timing System (STS), including dividends and interest, to the total return of the market itself on a buy and hold basis during the period.

In the table, the year is for the early May exit date of the seasonal system each year. The entry date is actually the late October seasonal entry of the previous fall. We have run the DJIA gains from the same date for accurate comparisons.

The table shows the gains made in each favorable period, which are obviously identical for both the Seasonal Timing System and the Dow Jones Industrial Average, since both are fully invested and receiving the same gains or losses, and the same dividends, during the period.

The differences occur during the unfavorable periods, when the DJIA experiences whatever gains or losses occur in the market, and collects the dividends for the period, while the STS is out of the market, missing out on market gains during the periods, missing out on the dividends, but also missing out on the losses that tend to occur during the unfavorable periods, *and* collecting interest on cash. I think you'll agree the performance difference is astounding.

YEAR	SEASON	DJIA AT STS ENTRY	DJIA AT STS EXIT	SEASONAL GAINS		COMPOUNDED GAIN	
				STS	DJIA	STS	DJIA
1964	Favorable	755.2	828.2	11.3%	11.3%	11.3%	11.3%
	Unfavorable			1.6%	6.9%	13.1%	19%
1965	Favorable	871.9	933.5	8.9%	8.9%	23.2%	29.6%
	Unfavorable			1.9%	4.6%	25.5%	35.6%
1966	Favorable	959.1	900	-4.5%	-4.5%	19.9%	29.5%
	Unfavorable			2.1%	-8.6%	22.4%	18.4%
1967	Favorable	808	901.9	13.5%	13.5%	38.9%	34.3%
	Unfavorable			2.3%	0.15%	42%	34.5%
1968	Favorable	886.6	914.5	4.9%	4.9%	48.9%	41%
	Unfavorable			2.2%	5.7%	52.2%	49.1%
1969	Favorable	951.1	962.1	2.9%	2.9%	56.6%	53.4%
	Unfavorable			2.8%	-9.9%	61%	38.3%
1970	Favorable	850.5	718.4	-13.6%	-13.6%	39.1%	19.5%
	Unfavorable			3.5%	6.8%	44%	27.7%
1971	Favorable	753.6	937.4	26.5%	26.5%	82.2%	61.6%
	Unfavorable			3.3%	-8.6%	88.1%	47.7%

YEAR	SEASON	DJIA AT STS ENTRY	DJIA AT STS EXIT	SEASONAL GAINS		COMPOUNDED GAIN	
				STS	DJIA	STS	DJIA
1972	Favorable	837.6	937.3	13.7%	13.7%	113.8%	67.9%
	Unfavorable			2.2%	2.7%	118.5%	72.5%
1973	Favorable	946.4	953.9	2.5%	2.5%	123.9%	76.8%
	Unfavorable			2.2%	3.2%	128.5%	82.5%
1974	Favorable	968.5	844.9	-10.9%	-10.9%	104%	62.7%
	Unfavorable			3.5%	-18.5%	111.1%	32.7%
1975	Favorable	673	834.7	26.5%	26.5%	167.1%	67.9%
	Unfavorable			3.8%	3.1%	177.2%	73%
1976	Favorable	839.4	989.5	20.2%	20.2%	233.2%	108%
	Unfavorable			3%	-1.4%	243.2%	105.1%
1977	Favorable	952.6	943.4	1.1%	1.1%	247.1%	107.4%
	Unfavorable			2.7%	-10.7%	256.3%	85.3%
1978	Favorable	822.7	824.4	2.8%	2.8%	266.1%	90.4%
	Unfavorable			2.6%	-1.5%	275.5%	87.6%
1979	Favorable	791.4	847.5	10%	10%	313.2%	106.4%
	Unfavorable			3.5%	.2%	327.6%	106.8%
1980	Favorable	823.8	816	2.1%	2.1%	336.4%	111%
	Unfavorable			5.3%	15.5%	359.3%	143.7%
1981	Favorable	917.8	973.3	9.1%	9.1%	401.1%	165.8%
	Unfavorable			5.6%	-11.4%	428.9%	135.6%
1982	Favorable	832.9	863.2	6.6%	6.6%	474%	151.2%
	Unfavorable			6.7%	17.8%	501.5%	196%
1983	Favorable	991	1220	26.1%	26.1%	658.7%	273.3%
	Unfavorable			5.4%	4.2%	699.3%	288.9%
1984	Favorable	1234	1165	-3.2%	-3.2%	673.7%	276.4%
	Unfavorable			4.3%	6.8%	707%	302.2%
1985	Favorable	1217	1248	5.1%	5.1%	747.8%	322.5%
	Unfavorable			4.9%	12.8%	788.9%	376.6%
1986	Favorable	1376	1788	32.3%	32.3%	1076%	530.6%
	Unfavorable			4%	7.4%	1124%	577.3%
1987	Favorable	1878	2342	26.5%	26.5%	1449%	757.1%
	Unfavorable			3.1%	-15.4%	1496%	625.1%
1988	Favorable	1938	2020	5.8%	5.8%	1588%	667%
	Unfavorable			3%	8%	1639%	728.2%

YEAR	SEASON	DJIA AT STS ENTRY	DJIA AT STS EXIT	SEASONAL GAINS		COMPOUNDED GAIN	
				STS	DJIA	STS	DJIA
1989	Favorable	2150	2385	12.9%	12.9%	1863%	834.9%
	Unfavorable			3.6%	11.1%	1932%	938.8%
1990	Favorable	2604	2710	6.2%	6.2%	2057%	1003%
	Unfavorable			4.1%	-7.6%	2146%	919%
1991	Favorable	2448	2942	22.2%	22.2%	2644%	1144%
	Unfavorable			3.6%	6.4%	2742%	1224%
1992	Favorable	3072	3369	11.1%	11.1%	3958%	1371%
	Unfavorable			2.8%	-2.2%	3144%	1338%
1993	Favorable	3246	3442	7.6%	7.6%	3392%	1448%
	Unfavorable			1.7%	8.8%	3451%	1583%
1994	Favorable	3688	3696	1.7%	1.7%	3510%	1611%
	Unfavorable			1.6%	7.8%	3566%	1744%
1995	Favorable	3931	4360	12.4%	12.4%	4020%	1973%
	Unfavorable			2.3%	10.6%	4115%	2191%
1996	Favorable	4757	5464	16.2%	16.2%	4798%	2563%
	Unfavorable			2.8%	11%	4936%	2857%
1997	Favorable	5993	7225	21.7%	21.7%	6029%	3499%
	Unfavorable			2.6%	3.3%	6188%	3618%
1998	Favorable	7382	9055	23.6%	23.6%	7670%	4494%
	Unfavorable			2.6%	-5.3%	**7872%**	**4252%**
1999	Favorable	8495					

Now we *really* have something! *Our Seasonal Timing System almost doubled the market on a buy and hold basis during the thirty-five-year period.* An investment of $100,000 would have grown to $7,872,000, whereas a buy and hold strategy would have turned $100,000 into only $4,252,000.

Even more astounding, higher performance usually requires taking more risk, but our Seasonal Timing System produced almost double the total return of the market with only 50 percent of the risk since the seasonal system was in the market only half the time.

Even more important, an investor would have no problem following the seasonal system since it solves all the problems of trying to follow a buy and hold strategy. Most important:

- It avoids the worst of the market's periodic plunges that make it difficult, in fact virtually impossible, for an investor to repeatedly hold through such painful periods.
- It eliminates the problem of the market that comes back from bear markets not being the same market each time because they keep changing stocks in the indexes. Each time the follower of the Seasonal Timing System reenters the market for the favorable period, he or she is buying whatever stocks compose the Index at the time.

EVEN FURTHER ENHANCEMENT

As impressive as the performance of our Seasonal Timing System is, we can make it even more so by adding a dash of *common sense*.

We'll use the next chart to illustrate. It shows the period from 1985 to 1989, chosen because it includes a variety of market activity, including the 1987 market crash. The chart is segmented to show the entry and exit points of the Seasonal Timing System.

To improve on the calendar date entries and exits of our Seasonal Timing System, you would simply check the market's action each evening for the week or two approaching the next anticipated calendar date, and use a little common sense.

For instance, look at the anticipated reentry point of October 29, 1987 (the day before the last trading day of October). The market was still declining in the aftermath of the market crash as the planned entry day approached. Common sense would tell you to postpone the entry until the decline stopped. As the saying goes, you don't want to step in and try to catch a falling knife. In this particular case, common sense

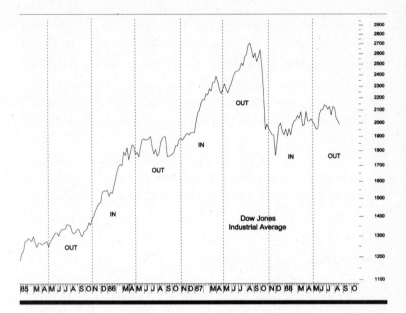

might have had you delay the reentry as much as a month. You'd simply wait until the market stopped going down and then put in several days of upside action. Given the gloomy prognostications in the media in the panicked aftermath of the market crash, I'll wager you would have had no problem letting common sense convince you to delay that particular reentry. The gloom from Wall Street was so thick the problem might even have become one of having enough courage to reenter at all. However, as the chart shows, having given none of your profits back in the crash as you were "out," your confidence in the system certainly should have remained high, and reentry should have been no problem.

As an example of enhancing the *exit* dates through common sense, look at the market action as the early May exit dates in 1985, 1986, 1987, and 1988 approached. The market began declining for several days before the date arrived. If you were going to exit on May 4 anyway, and the market started losing ground on April 26, or April 27, common sense would tell you there's no percentage in holding on until the specific date to exit.

There's no way to quantify how much simple common sense would enhance the entry and exit points. Everyone would have different timing each time as to when to react to the short-term market action. However, it's obvious that common sense could well increase gains by several percentage points annually. Compounded over the long term, the difference would be significant.

One caution: there is risk if you start second-guessing the "specific date" seasonal system by more than just a week or so if your only tool is commonsense observance of the market's short-term activity.

A STAND-ALONE SYSTEM

Our Enhanced Seasonal Timing System at this point is perfectly capable of standing alone. Its tools and rules are certainly simple, and far easier to stick with during both sides of market cycles than a buy and hold strategy.

1. Buy a good legible calendar.
2. Sell on the fourth trading day of May and go away! Forget the market! Travel. Play golf.
3. Come back in October. Reenter on the day before the last trading day of the month.
4. Forget the market again. Don't watch it. Don't fret about its gyrations. Enjoy Thanksgiving, Christmas, New Years. Go skiing.
5. Come back in April. Repeat steps 2 through 4.

I don't want to mislead you. There has never been a totally perfect system and never will be. Our new Enhanced Seasonal Timing System does not avoid *all* the market's volatility. As shown in the tables, there have been a few years, a very few, when the market has declined during its favorable November to May period. There have also been years when the market made good gains in its unfavorable period, which a follower of the system would have missed. So there were occasions when an investor would be exiting in May at a lower price than when he or she entered the previous November, or would be reentering in November at a higher price than he or she exited in May.

The system's remarkable long-term performance is produced by the numerous occasions when the market does underperform during the unfavorable period. Some of those declines set the market back so much it took several years for it to get back to where it was prior to the decline.

However, the system is still not perfect. *The upside of that is that anything that's not perfect can still be improved upon.*

Before we go further, I need to say that the Enhanced Seasonal Timing System, enhanced further by the application of some degree of common sense at the actual entries and exits, is an excellent investment strategy for the majority of investors, and as far into market timing as the majority of investors should go, or need to go.

Almost doubling the total return of the market with such ease, and with half the risk of being fully invested all the time, is an astounding achievement. Just *matching* the total return of the market as measured by the Dow or S&P 500 is normally a difficult task. Few money managers do so. Even fewer mutual fund managers do so. Yet they are *full-time*, trained, experienced professionals.

The majority of working investors are busy with their careers, as they should be since that's the area of *their* expertise and experience, and the source of their investment capital. So, since our Enhanced Seasonal Timing System promises not to just match the market, but to substantially outperform the market, and does so with half the market's risk, most investors should just take that information, pass it along to family members and friends they care about, and run to the bank, or their brokers (depending on the season), with a smile on their face.

CHAPTER 8

ADDING A TECHNICAL INDICATOR

For those with the time and inclination to go further, it's obvious that rally tops will not occur exactly on the fourth trading day of May every year, or even any year, and correction bottoms will not take place exactly on the second day before the end of October every year, or even any year. All the system is doing is playing the very significant odds that the bulk of most rallies will take place within the seasonally favorable time frames, that the monthly strength period will add several percentage points each year, and that interest earned on cash in the unfavorable periods will beat the market during those periods in most years.

Obviously, from the numbers, that's all that's necessary. And why not? After all, having the odds only slightly in the house's favor is all it takes over the long term to produce the huge profits of Las Vegas casinos. Shifting the odds back the other way a small amount, by illegally "counting" the cards as they're played, is all it takes for a blackjack player to clean out the house.

Our next step is to find a way to move our exits and entrances more closely to the actual tops and bottoms of the market trends that are underway at the time of the calendar date entries and exits. Using common sense may be as good a way as any to go, but there's no way to measure the results. In addition, using a few simple market timing indicators should give us a wider range in which to safely make the moves.

MORE THAN JUST A CALENDAR

Keep the goals in mind. We're not trying to become day traders, or hedge fund operators, or market analysts. We simply want to pinpoint entry and exit points for the seasonal system more closely than simply using calendar dates. To achieve that goal, we do not need to become full-fledged market timers, but we do need to use more than just a calendar, and need to have a bit more knowledge of how the market operates than many investors bother to accumulate.

Unfortunately, that means if you're going to reap the benefit, you're just going to have to put up with a few pages of what investors hate: statistics and explanations.

ADDING AN ACTUAL MARKET TIMING TOOL

There are hundreds of technical and fundamental indicators, as well as methods of analysis, used by professionals in timing the market's ups and downs.

It used to be in the old days, prior to the introduction of affordable computers and the development of charting software in the 1980s, that we had to keep charts and technical indicators updated manually. That forced us to keep it simple and focused, on just the time-proven indicators and techniques. The introduction of personal computers and charting software gave everyone the ability to instantly generate hundreds of charts and indicators, far more than could possibly be wisely combined to form an overall expectation for market direction. However, investors thought they'd found the Holy Grail. The ability to generate charts would make them instant market timers. Indeed, the software was promoted as having that magic power.

Investors soon discovered the production of charts was simply a clerical function the computer had replaced. The magic was still in understanding the markets, and being able to interpret what a combination of charts was saying in relation to all the surrounding conditions that affect the market. The proliferation of hundreds of different types of indicators, simultaneously pointing in different directions depending on what they were measuring, and the time frame they were focused on, only added to their confusion.

However, to move up another level in improving the entry and exit points of the seasonal system, even though we're going to keep it simple, you'll need the use of a personal computer, a program for downloading basic market data from a data source, and a minimal software program to generate a chart of the market and the one or two indicators we'll be using.

I'm using Equis International's state-of-the-art Metastock Professional package for the charts and indicators in this chapter. It sells for $1475, and includes a program that allows you to download market data via a telephone modem or over the Internet. You would need maybe 1 percent of its capabilities for the simple charting we'll be using to enhance the entry and exit points of our Enhanced Seasonal Timing System.

At the other end of the spectrum, some brokerage firms provide free software that will provide the simple charting needed, and you can update manually at no cost, by entering the small amount of data we'll be using right out of the daily newspaper each evening. In choosing a software package, just check to make sure it will produce the few indicators detailed in the following discussion.

TIMING THE VERY SHORT-TERM TREND

As mentioned, we're not trying to be market timers. We're interested only in something that has a good chance of telling us twice a year whether the market is in a short-term rally at the time or in a short-term pullback. We don't need, or even want, something that would attempt to tell us what the market will do intermediate term or at some other time of the year. That would only tempt us to deviate from the seasonal system and go off on some cockamamie chase.

A chart of the market's action in 1986 is shown here. It has two inner windows. The lower window shows the Dow Jones

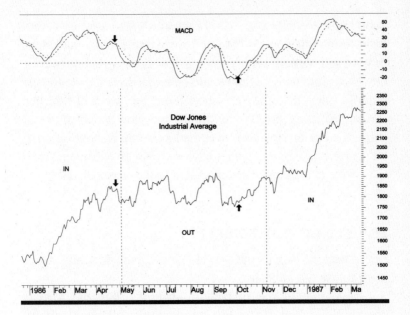

Industrial Average (DJIA), and the upper window shows the short term MACD indicator.

The MACD (Moving Average Convergence Divergence) indicator is a momentum reversal indicator developed many years ago by Gerald Appel of the Signalert Corporation. There are several variations, but basically, it consists of two moving averages, one slow moving, the other faster moving. You don't need to know its formula since your charting software will simply spit the chart out on demand.

However, you do need to know how the indicator triggers buy and sell signals. When the solid line of the indicator is below the dotted trigger line, and then moves up to cross the trigger line, the indicator produces a buy signal. When the solid line of the indicator is above the dotted trigger line and then crosses the trigger line to the downside, a sell signal is produced.

Before we go any further, let me say you have not just been introduced to something that will transform you into an ace market timer. This indicator has its purposes. It also has severe limitations. We are using it as a very short-term indicator by applying it to daily data. As the chart shows, used as a very short-term indicator it is "timing" every ripple in the market, its buy or sell signals lasting only a few days to a few weeks. Obviously, the whipsawing would be brutal were it used for any purpose other than the very short term. Yet, we will find that sometimes its reversals will still be too slow to enhance our entries and exits. However, over the long term, it should keep us on the right side of the market longer at enough entries and exits to provide considerable enhancement to the seasonal system.

TO SELL OR NOT TO SELL

Let's check its signals out over a few cycles historically, as we learn to use the indicator.

Note that in the first chart, that of 1986, the MACD crossed the dotted trigger line, producing a sell signal, almost two weeks before our anticipated seasonal exit of the fourth trading day in May. (The anticipated calendar dates for exits and entrances are at the vertical dotted lines.) The Dow closed at 1894 the day after the sell signal, the day we would have acted on the signal. If we had waited until the calendar exit on the fourth trading day of May, we would have exited at a considerably lower price since the Dow closed at 1788 that day.

Note that as we then approached the anticipated reentry in late October, the MACD produced a short-term buy signal early in October when the solid line moved up to cross the dotted trigger line, on October 6. If we entered the following day, we would have entered with the Dow at 1784. If we had instead waited for the seasonal system's calendar date entry of the day before the last trading day in October, we would have entered with the Dow at 1878.

So, as you can see, we are talking about the potential for yet another significant enhancement to the Seasonal Timing System through the addition of just one very simple technical indicator.

Let's look at another period as the 1990's bull market was getting underway.

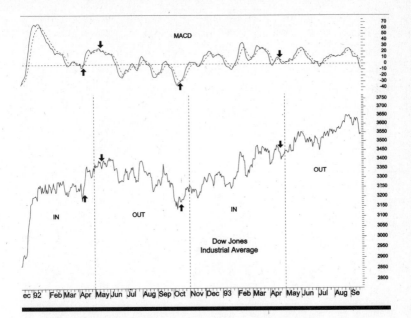

The seasonal timing worked out fine, but the MACD gave us mixed performance this time as an enhancement over the calendar dates (which are represented by the vertical dotted lines). As the May 1992 exit approached, the MACD triggered a buy signal, which helped us by delaying our exit. The subsequent reentry in October was also improved when another buy signal from the MACD called for entering two weeks before the calendar date entry would have put us in. However, at the subsequent exit the following May, an MACD sell signal gave us a lower exit price than we would have received had we waited for the calendar exit date.

Lastly, we'll show you a chart of a quite volatile market period, that from late 1996 to late 1998, when investors in the unusually one-sided bull market of the 1990s experienced the first return of normal up *and* down volatility since 1990.

On this chart, at the exit from the favorable period in May 1997, the MACD was on a clear buy signal, and the market was clearly rallying as the exit date approached. By waiting to exit until MACD triggered a sell signal, we made a nice additional gain.

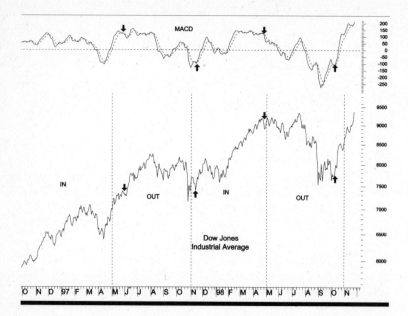

At the next anticipated entry in late October 1997, the MACD was on a sell signal as the entry date approached. By waiting until the MACD triggered a buy signal a few days after the normal calendar entry date, we entered at a higher price, losing ground. At the subsequent exit in early May 1998, we also lost some ground since a sell signal on the MACD before the calendar exit date got us out at a somewhat lower price than had we waited for the calendar date exit.

However, after the Seasonal Timing System kept us out for the entire significant 1998 correction, a buy signal on the MACD in mid-October then provided an entry a full 557 points better than had we waited for the calendar date.

I've deliberately chosen charts where the MACD was not always a helpful addition to the system so that you will realize it will not always give better entries and exits. Knowing that, and realizing it is only the long-term results that count, I hope you will not let an inferior signal, or two in a row, cause you to abandon the system.

THE RESULTS

The following table is identical to the last table (on page 69) that compared the Seasonal Timing System to being fully invested in the DJIA, except rather than using the calendar dates of the system, we've changed the entries and exits of the STS to the day after nearby signals were triggered on the MACD indicator.

You'll note that also changes the gains and losses of the DJIA for each period, since the MACD provides different holding periods, and we are comparing the performance of both the STS and the DJIA in each period.

Performance of STS Enhanced by MACD Entries and Exits

YEAR	SEASON	DJIA AT STS ENTRY	DJIA AT STS EXIT	SEASONAL GAINS		COMPOUNDED GAIN	
				STS	DJIA	STS	DJIA
1964	Favorable	750.6	823	11.3%	11.3%	11.3%	11.3%
	Unfavorable			1.6%	9.6%	13.1%	22%
1965	Favorable	888.7	932.1	6.7%	6.7%	20.7%	30.2%
	Unfavorable			1.9%	4.5%	23%	36%
1966	Favorable	956.3	932	-0.9%	-0.9%	21.9%	34.8%
	Unfavorable			2.1%	-14.8%	24.5%	14.9%
1967	Favorable	778.9	890	16.1%	16.1%	44.5%	33.4%
	Unfavorable			2.3%	-0.3%	47.8%	33%
1968	Favorable	870.9	918.9	7.2%	7.2%	58.5%	42.6%
	Unfavorable			2.2%	5%	62%	49.8%
1969	Favorable	949.6	951.8	2%	2%	65.2%	52.8%
	Unfavorable			2.8%	-10.1%	69.8%	37.3%
1970	Favorable	838.8	782.6	-4.8%	-4.8%	61.7%	30.8%
	Unfavorable			3.5%	0.6%	67.4%	31.6%
1971	Favorable	772	932.4	22.9%	22.9%	105.7%	61.7%
	Unfavorable			3.3%	-8.9%	112.4%	47.2%
1972	Favorable	829.7	957.4	17.1%	17.1%	148.8%	72.5%
	Unfavorable			2.2%	1.1%	154.3%	74.4%
1973	Favorable	951.4	937.8	0.3%	0.3%	154.9%	74.9%
	Unfavorable			2.2%	-9.4%	160.6%	58.5%

YEAR	SEASON	DJIA AT STS ENTRY	DJIA AT STS EXIT	SEASONAL GAINS		COMPOUNDED GAIN	
				STS	DJIA	STS	DJIA
1974	Favorable	834.2	834.6	2%	2%	165.6%	61.6%
	Unfavorable			3.5%	-20.5%	174.9%	28.6%
1975	Favorable	648	831	30.7%	30.7%	259.4%	68.1%
	Unfavorable			3.7%	2.6%	272.9%	72.5%
1976	Favorable	832	986.5	20.9%	20.9%	350.9%	108.6%
	Unfavorable			3%	-1.1%	364.5%	106.3%
1977	Favorable	952.6	923.8	-0.9%	-0.9%	360.2%	104.4%
	Unfavorable			2.6%	-9.3%	372.4%	85.4%
1978	Favorable	818.4	822	3%	3%	386.5%	90.9%
	Unfavorable			2.6%	-1.9%	398.9%	87.3%
1979	Favorable	785.3	857.9	12.2%	12.2%	459.7%	110.1%
	Unfavorable			3.5%	2.3%	479.3%	105.2%
1980	Favorable	812.6	869.7	10%	10%	537.4%	125.8%
	Unfavorable			5.3%	12.3%	570.9%	153.6%
1981	Favorable	950.7	995.6	7.8%	7.8%	623%	173.3%
	Unfavorable			5.6%	-11.5%	663.1%	141.8%
1982	Favorable	850.6	854.4	3.5%	3.5%	689.5%	150.1%
	Unfavorable			6.6%	18.5%	742%	196.4%
1983	Favorable	986.8	1218	26.6%	26.6%	965.5%	275.1%
	Unfavorable			5.3%	5.5%	1022%	296%
1984	Favorable	1248	1157	-4.9%	-4.9%	967%	276%
	Unfavorable			4.3%	5.7%	1013%	297%
1985	Favorable	1196	1242	6.4%	6.4%	1084%	323%
	Unfavorable			4.9%	9.6%	1141%	363%
1986	Favorable	1329	1894	44.9%	44.9%	1699%	571%
	Unfavorable			4%	-3.5%	1771%	548%
1987	Favorable	1784	2287	30%	30%	2334%	743%
	Unfavorable			3%	-13.1%	2408%	632%
1988	Favorable	1945	2003	4.5%	4.5%	2522%	665%
	Unfavorable			3%	7.7%	2600%	724%
1989	Favorable	2126	2376	13.7%	13.7%	2970%	837%
	Unfavorable			3.6%	3.6%	3079%	948%
1990	Favorable	2610	2696	5.4%	5.4%	3249%	1004%
	Unfavorable			4.1%	-4.6%	3387%	953%

YEAR	SEASON	DJIA AT STS ENTRY	DJIA AT STS EXIT	SEASONAL GAINS		COMPOUNDED GAIN	
				STS	DJIA	STS	DJIA
1991	Favorable	2516	2912	17.7%	17.7%	4005%	1140%
	Unfavorable			3.6%	6.8%	4153%	1225%
1992	Favorable	3053	3398	12.7%	12.7%	4693%	1393%
	Unfavorable			2.7%	-4.8%	4825%	1321%
1993	Favorable	3187	3398	8.2%	8.2%	5230%	1438%
	Unfavorable			1.7%	7%	5320%	1546%
1994	Favorable	3583	3783	7%	7%	5701%	1662%
	Unfavorable			1.6%	5.2%	5791%	1753%
1995	Favorable	3923	4436	14.5%	14.5%	6647%	2021%
	Unfavorable			2.3%	8.6%	6802%	2205%
1996	Favorable	4755	5549	18%	18%	8048%	2621%
	Unfavorable			2.8%	10.5%	8276%	2908%
1997	Favorable	6059	7383	23%	23%	10,203%	3600%
	Unfavorable			2.6%	4.8%	10,471%	3776%
1998	Favorable	7650	9064	19.4%	19.4%	11,149%	4025%
	Unfavorable			2.6%	-1%	11,441%	3994%
1999	Favorable	7938	11,007	39.4%	39.4%	17,905%	5508%

All right! The addition of the simple MACD indicator made another substantial improvement in the Seasonal Timing System, now almost tripling the total return of the DJIA on a buy and hold basis.

Note also that the worst "drawdown" suffered by the Seasonal Timing System was 5 percent in 1984. *That compares to the eleven serious corrections or bear markets encountered by the DJIA on a buy and hold basis during the period, with declines as large as 45 percent, and averaging 26 percent.*

Even in the unprecedented bull market of the 1990s, the STS captures most of the gains as they did take place during the "favorable" period each year.

CAUTION: The performance in the Table cannot be compared to the market's historic calendar year performances. The "Year" in the Table runs from October to October, from the

MACD triggered entry date of the previous fall to the next entry after the unfavorable period ends in October of the year shown.

CONCLUSION

We combined two impressive *seasonal* tendencies, each having impressive historical performance, one of six-month duration, one of short-term duration. Just that combination resulted in a Seasonal Timing System that over at least the last thirty-five years outperformed the market to an extraordinary degree, almost doubling the return of the market on a buy and hold basis, including dividends.

Then we added a short-term momentum indicator, the MACD, that has the job of moving the calendar entry dates closer to the bottom of corrections and the exit points closer to the top of rallies that may be underway as the calendar dates approach. That enhancement added still more gains, almost tripling the return of the market on a buy and hold basis.

Yet, the extraordinary performance is achieved, not with more risk, not with the same risk, but with 50 percent of the prevailing risk in any market year.

Obviously, the new Enhanced Seasonal Timing System works through both bull and bear markets. In fact, it makes no effort to determine whether the market is in a bull or bear phase.

The Enhanced Seasonal Timing System, even on just a calendar basis, provides a simple method for any investor to safely ride both bull and bear markets, beating not only buy and hold investors by a country mile, but also the majority of professional market timers and money managers! And it does so without breaking a sweat about being mauled repeatedly by the angry bear.

Do we really need to go any further? How greedy should we get?

. . . Okay. I get the picture. Let's get all we can.

CHAPTER 9

STILL MORE PROFITS— FROM A BEAR

Would you believe that bear markets are *best*? Here's the key. Markets go down *at least* three times as fast as they go up!

For example, any gains made between 1958 and 1973, assuming one bought in 1958, and held through thick and thin, were totally wiped out in the bear market of 1973–1974, which lasted just two years. One would have made as many Dow points on the downturn, in just two years, as were made in fifteen years in the previous uptrend.

More recently, in the brief 1987 bear market, the Dow declined 984 points, or 36.1 percent in two months. It had taken the previous eighteen months to gain those 984 points. Gains could have been made from the bear market nine times as fast as the gains made in the previous bull market.

Similarly, the brief 1990 bear market was over in just three months. It wiped out gains that had taken fourteen months to achieve. Looked at from the other direction, for short sellers the market achieved fourteen months of gains in just three months.

Since on average a bear market moves *at least* three times as fast as a bull market, bear markets can produce profits at least three times as fast as a bull market if we harness their power.

USING A BEAR TO IMPROVE THE SEASONAL TIMING SYSTEM

As beneficial as the Seasonal Timing System is by itself, it's aimed only at keeping investors standing aside in cash during the

87

unfavorable periods that are most likely to encompass market declines. Imagine what we would accomplish if, instead of just standing aside with our profits when the market is going down, we were able to make additional gains *from* the market decline.

Of course, the first question is how could we possibly make *gains* in a declining market? A bull market is a market where we make profits, and a bear market is a decline that takes back those profits. Right?

The arrogant maxim of corporate America that "Bear markets are when stocks are returned to their rightful owners" might make us believe that. Corporate America, wealthy investors, and Wall Street professionals do believe that most public investors can be enticed into piling into stocks at the high prices near market tops. They believe public investors can then be convinced to try to hold those high-priced stocks through subsequent bear markets, but will always give up at the lows, and "return" the stocks to those from whom they bought them—but at much lower prices.

Well, we already have a system to defeat that nonsense, the Seasonal Timing System, which should have us, like them, selling to take profits when prices are high and buying them back when prices are low. The STS also provides us with the cash at the beginning of the unfavorable periods with which to make gains from the downside. But how do we go about it?

The process of profiting from a serious market correction, or bear market, is very similar to making profits in a bull market.

In bull markets, we make gains by buying a stock when its price is low and holding it while we wait for the price to rise. The process is known as holding a "long position." When the price has risen sufficiently, we sell the stock to take the profit and close out the position.

In the case of mutual funds, we buy funds that are invested in a diversified portfolio of stocks that are expected to rise in price.

The main difference in making profits from a bear market is that to profit from a stock that's declining in price, we reverse the order in which we buy it low and sell it high. That is, by a process that's known as selling the stock short, we actually sell the stock first, at a high price, and buy it later, we hope at a lower price.

SELLING SHORT

Most investors are only vaguely familiar with the term "selling short" or, having heard it described, believe it's too complicated for them. The fact is the procedure is neither complicated nor that much different from their normal process of *buying* stocks in bull markets.

How can we sell a stock before we own it? We don't have the asset (we're short of it) and yet we can sell it? Yes, we can.

Although it's necessary to know how it works, we don't want to get too hung up on the mechanics of the process. After all, in taking a long position, few investors understand the various procedures that are involved. They simply place an order to buy a stock and leave the rest to their brokerage firm. Yet their stock may be purchased for them through the stock's specialist in the floor auction on the NYSE, on one of the eight other regional stock exchanges, from a broker-dealer in the computerized NASDAQ system, from their brokerage firm's own inventory, or even as part of a secondary offering of the stock. The investor doesn't know, or need to know, the details.

In selling short, the investor simply tells the broker he or she wants to sell 100 shares of XYZ company short. The broker will report the price received and the proceeds of the sale. The proceeds (the cash from the sale) will be placed in the investor's account just like the sale of any stock. The investor will then be holding a short position in the stock. How was the investor able to sell stock he or she didn't own? The broker borrowed 100 shares of the stock for the investor, either from the brokerage firm's inventory or from another investor's account, and sold those shares, placing the cash in the investor's account. Since it's a loan of the shares, the investor will pay interest on their value as long as the loan is outstanding. However, the investor will also receive interest on the cash that comes into his or her account from the sale of the shares.

When the investor tells the broker he or she wants to close the short position, ideally because the shares have fallen in price as he or she expected, the broker will buy 100 shares of XYZ company at its current price. The broker will then return those shares to his or her firm's inventory or the other investor's account from which they were originally borrowed. The short position is thus closed out.

If the broker originally borrowed 100 shares of XYZ stock to sell short for the investor, and sold them at $100 a share, the investor took in $10,000. If the stock then declines in price to $60 per share, he or she pays out only $6000 when the broker buys 100 shares to return to the account from which they were borrowed. The $4000 difference remains in the investor's account and is his or her profit (minus interest and commissions).

MUTUAL FUNDS THAT MAKE MONEY IN A BEAR MARKET

In our newsletter, although we provide both a recommended mutual fund portfolio and an equities portfolio, we have always advised that most investors should stick with mutual funds.

The reasons are many.

Mutual funds provide instant diversification among a significant number of stocks. In the case of no-load funds, they can be purchased and sold without paying commissions or fees. They can be entered, or switched to cash, with just one quick phone call. Only the fund needs to be analyzed and followed by the investor, not the stocks within the fund. Last but not least, mutual funds have their stock holdings chosen by professional managers, who not only always receive information on companies sooner than public investors, but also have access to hot new issues and other investments that small investors just cannot buy.

Those advantages were understood, but subscribers would ask how mutual funds could be used to make profits when the next prolonged bear market of several years duration arrives? At least by sticking with individual stocks, an investor could switch to selling stocks short.

It was an excellent question. The only answer we could give was that the securities industry is very adaptive to changing needs, and we were sure that when conditions began to set up for a prolonged bear market, mutual funds for such conditions would be available.

That has come to pass. A growing number of such funds have been introduced in recent years, funds designed to make money *only* in down markets. They primarily hold short positions and put options (which make leveraged gains when the market declines), while limiting their long positions, if any, to sectors they expect will make gains when the general market is in decline, perhaps gold, real estate investment trusts, utilities, or bonds.

Other mutual funds have arrived on the scene that are designed to move *directly* opposite to the stock market. For instance, the aptly named Rydex Ursa fund invests in S&P 500 futures contracts in a manner designed to move the fund in the opposite direction to the stock market as measured by the S&P 500. That is, if the S&P 500 gains 40 percent, this fund is designed so that it will lose 40 percent. It's therefore not a fund either to buy and hold or to own in a bull market. However, in a period when the S&P 500 *declines* 40 percent, the fund is designed to *gain* 40 percent, making it an ideal fund to hold in a bear market.

BEAR FUNDS TURN OUT TO BE CUBS

Yet, though we believe strongly that mutual funds are the way to go in bull markets, it has turned out that investors *would* be better off selling individual stocks short in bear markets rather than using bear-market-type mutual funds.

The reason is that in bull markets, mutual funds that are designed for up markets are going to be *fully invested* for the upside, and their managers will have better odds of putting together a portfolio of winning stocks than will individual investors. However, our study of the bear market funds shows that as part of their defensive positioning, most hold high levels of cash, and so are not fully invested for the downside. Of the portion they have invested, in addition to short positions, they also tend to hold long positions in areas they believe will not be hurt as badly in a bear market, and that *may* even make gains in a down market.

Obviously, the high level of cash and the defensive-type long positions significantly dilute the effect of the short positions.

In the case of bear-market-type funds that are designed to move opposite to an index such as the S&P 500, those market indexes consist of the largest, most stable "blue chip" stocks. They will therefore always, as a group, decline less than the rest of the market when the market is in a correction. It's not unusual for the average stock in the broad market to be down 35 percent when the S&P 500 is down only 20 percent, or for the average stock to be down 60 percent when the S&P 500 is down 40 percent.

Therefore, we advise going after profits in a bear market, or in a serious correction, by zeroing in on individual "overvalued" stocks through the use of short sales. Such positions will not be diluted and will be aimed at fully utilizing the potential of the declining market.

So, if we are in agreement that we should go after further gains rather than just standing aside in cash during serious market declines, let's plan our hunting trip.

BEARS MOSTLY HIBERNATE

We already know that, the unusual bull market of the 1990s notwithstanding, bull markets last an average of 26.6 months. Therefore, we know that every May exit of our Seasonal Timing System is *not* going to be followed by a bear market. Sometimes unfavorable periods will see only minor pullbacks or sideways market action or even further upside activity.

So, we need a means of measuring market risk once a year, as each favorable period draws to a close, so that we can go after gains from the downside only in those years when odds are high that an unfavorable period will launch a bear market or serious decline.

The tools to make that determination are available.

We're halfway there because we already know we *must* ignore the self-serving propaganda from Wall Street since that would have us believe the market is *never* at high risk.

LOOKING FOR BEAR SIGNS

Norman Cousins, former famed editor of *The Saturday Review*, provided an excellent starting point for us when he pointed out that, "History is a vast early warning system."

Our starting point will therefore be in the historical statistics that tell us what conditions were in place when bear markets began in the past. Once we know that similar conditions are in place as any favorable seasonal period draws to a close, and a serious correction or bear market is likely, we can zero in on individual stocks that are overvalued, where the company's "insiders" are selling, and where our momentum indicators tell us the stock has rolled over into a correction.

IGNORE THE CROWD

The first thing to take from the historical data we're going to explore is that conditions that accompany market tops (and correction bottoms) are diametrically opposed to popular notions. As we learned in earlier chapters, investors and analysts tend to extend the current market trend in a straight line into the future, becoming increasingly more convinced it will last forever. Following crowd psychology will therefore *never* prepare us for a change in market direction *in either direction* until it's far too late. So, it's extremely important to ignore what the majority are saying about market conditions at any particular time.

We must obtain and analyze *only* facts, and not be swayed by the emotions of the crowd or what sounds like reasoned analysis. As Joe Friday used to say, "Just give us the facts, ma'am."

THE MARKET CAN ONLY GO UP

For example, Wall Street spokespeople propped up investor confidence at the market top in 1998, keeping investors buying with the Dow at 9300, with assurances that the bull market was at no risk and these are direct quotes:

"The current very low inflation rate can only be extremely bullish for the market. Only if high inflation returns some time in the future would we begin to worry about the market, as high inflation would cut into corporate earnings."

"Investors need not worry about the bull market ending with interest rates this low."

"The unemployment rate is at a 20-year low, and consumer confidence is at a record high. The economy and stock market cannot top out under such bullish conditions."

The media picked up on such "analysis" and the theories soon dominated market discussions around the water cooler and over cocktails, and became dogma.

However, the market *did* top out, in April 1998, and by September the average stock on the NYSE was down more than 30 percent, the NASDAQ was down 30 percent, the Transportation average was down 36 percent, and the S&P 500 was down 19½ percent. Investors were beginning to panic.

What was wrong with Wall Street's claims that the market could only go up as long as inflation and interest rates remained low and consumer confidence remained high? The claims were diametrically opposite to the historical facts.

For example, the following table shows how those economic, monetary, and consumer sentiment levels of 1998 compared to their levels in 1982. Keep in mind that in 1982 a bear market was just *ending*, and a big bull market was about to launch, making it one of the best buying opportunities ever.

	AUGUST 1982	AUGUST 1998
Inflation Rate (Consumer Price Index)	6.4%	3.0%
Unemployment Rate	9.8%	4.7%
Consumer Confidence Index	57	132
Interest Rates (30-Year-bond)	13.3%	5.2%

High inflation, *high* unemployment, *high* interest rates, and *low* consumer confidence were the conditions present at that excellent buying opportunity in 1982, not the opposite conditions that Wall Street was touting as bullish in 1998.

Looking back at other market turning points, inflation was at its second highest level *ever* in 1974. Was high inflation bad for the market that time? Definitely not. That was the bottom of the severe 1973–1974 bear market, another of the best buying opportunities of all time.

On the other hand, let's look at previous important market *tops*, when serious bear markets were about to begin. The last time the unemployment rate was as low as 4.7 percent was in 1973, just as the severe 1973–1974 bear market *began*. The last time consumer confidence reached 130 was in 1969, just as the 1969–1970 bear market began. Yet, in 1998, Wall Street was telling us those very same conditions were bullish for the market.

The following chart, courtesy of Ned Davis Research Inc., also clearly shows that it is high unemployment, not low, that has marked important buying opportunities, particularly in 1949, 1954, 1958, 1962, 1971, 1975, 1983, and 1993. The chart also shows that unemployment tended to reach its lows for each cycle *as the market was topping out.*

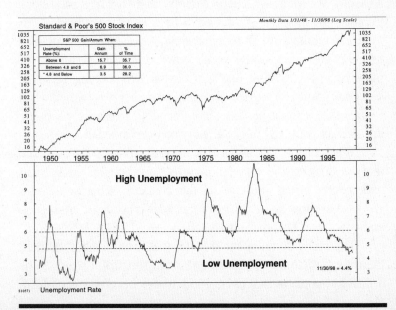

Wall Street's claims don't even pass the commonsense hurdle. Obviously, full employment and high consumer confidence would be in place only after a long period of good times, when the market would already have made significant gains and be more likely to be near a *top* than a good buying opportunity. On the other hand, common sense tells us that *high* unemployment and *low* consumer confidence would be more likely to accompany the good buying opportunities since those conditions would be more likely at correction lows, after a period of bad times. The historical statistics confirm that.

So, we'll ignore what Wall Street tells us and look elsewhere for measurements of whether the market is in a low risk or a high risk zone as an unfavorable seasonal period approaches.

STOCK VALUATIONS

Stock valuation seems to be one of the biggest stumbling blocks individual investors have regarding their understanding of the market. One of the questions I'm most often asked is why a stock they want to buy in a good company they're familiar with, maybe a Disney, WalMart, or General Motors, might not be a good stock to buy at the moment. If the stock's been in a nice rally, it seems to be even more difficult to understand. As one person explained to me, "The stock is not going down. It's been going up for months. I would think that's just what I'm looking for. And everyone knows it's a good company." Another was baffled when I suggested a stock he was recommending "because it's going up, already doubled" might already be overvalued.

When I try to talk about how the rising price is the problem, that the stock has become temporarily "overbought," or overvalued, people often can't grasp the concept. What sometimes works is to show them a chart of the stock's history of trading up and down as it becomes alternately oversold and overbought.

Then they do understand better that even in a bull market, there's a time to buy and a time to wait. But still it seems to be a difficult concept that even good stocks become overvalued,

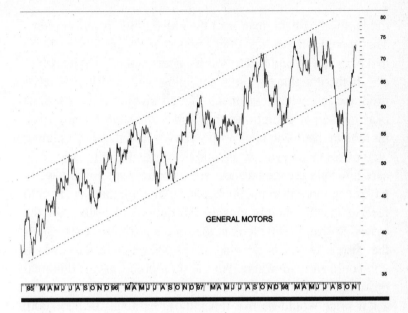

GENERAL MOTORS

that is, get ahead of their earnings, and either pull back while their earnings catch up, a healthy pattern, or become continuously more overvalued until a severe collapse is all that will carry them back to "fair value" levels.

The most common method of measuring the degree to which stocks are overvalued or undervalued is to compare the price of the stock to the company's earnings, book value, and dividend yield.

LET'S BUY A DONUT SHOP

The situation is not unlike the valuation process you'd go through if, rather than buying part of a publicly traded company, you were thinking of buying a small private business, perhaps a local coffee and doughnut shop. You'd first want to know the doughnut shop's book value, which is the value of its assets minus its debts. The assets might include the building the shop is in, the doughnut-making equipment, and the inventory of coffee beans and dough. The debt might be a mortgage on the building, a bank loan, and the unpaid bills from suppliers. That would tell you the shop's underlying value if you didn't make a go of it, and had to sell its assets and pay off its debts.

If the doughnut shop is not doing well, and the owner is tired and just wants out, much like an investor after a serious bear market, you might be able to buy the shop for not much more than that basic book value. However, if the shop is doing well under its present owner, and he or she doesn't particularly care how quickly the business sells, chances are you'll have to pay much more than the book value. After all, the owner could receive that by simply closing the doors and selling off the assets. So, you'll next look at the shop's profits, or earnings. If the current owner is drawing a $35,000 annual salary, which you could earn anywhere, but the shop produces an additional profit of $50,000 after taxes, you might reach an agreement that a fair price would be five times those earnings, or $250,000, plus the value of the building. On that basis, it would take five years of profits to pay for the business before you would begin to receive the profits for yourself. Other factors would also enter the valuation process. For instance, if you see ways to increase the profit after you take over, perhaps because you have a recipe for a special doughnut, or ideas for attracting more customers, you'll be willing to pay a bit more.

CARRYING DONUTS TO WALL STREET

Arriving at the fair value of a publicly traded company is a similar process. Analysts look at the company's book value, or underlying assets minus debts. Sometimes those assets can be the biggest factor in arriving at a value for the company's stock. For instance, the amount of gold a mining company still has in the ground may be of more importance in coming up with a fair price for its stock than the earnings the company is presently making from its mining operations. A timber company's stock, or an agricultural company's stock, may be valued more for the worth of their acreage than for the earnings they're producing from their operations.

However, just as with small private businesses, it's a publicly traded company's earnings and prospects for future earnings that carry the most weight in coming up with a fair value for its stock at any given moment. And it's the multiple of those earnings that investors are willing to pay at any moment that most determines whether a stock is selling at fair value, at undervalued levels, or at overvalued levels.

PRICE/EARNINGS RATIOS

If a company's earnings are stable, neither growing nor contracting, analysts may decide that ten times earnings is a fair price for its stock. However, if something happens that causes analysts to expect the company's earnings will rise substantially over coming years, they'll apply additional value to that prospect, and perhaps determine that the company's stock is worth, not ten times the company's present earnings, but ten times the higher earnings the company is likely to achieve the following year. Just as the prospective buyer of a doughnut shop would pay somewhat more knowing he or she could earn more from the shop than the present owner is earning, so a buyer of a piece of a public company would willingly pay more if he or she believes the company will achieve higher earnings going forward.

As time passes, and a company meets or exceeds the earnings that analysts had estimated for it, and the company's prospects continue to look good, analysts will increasingly ratchet up their earnings estimates for coming years. *If the company's stock price grew only at a pace that kept the stock selling at ten times those growing earnings, the stock would never become overvalued* (unless the company ran into problems and the earnings began to decline).

However, as we've already learned, investors become very enthusiastic in bull markets and become more concerned about being left behind by the rising prices than they are with the price they're paying to own a piece of a business. So as a bull market continues, a company that was selling at ten times its estimated earnings for the following year may soon be selling at fifteen times those earnings, then twenty times, twenty-five times. In the process, the stock first trades somewhat above its fair value, but reasonably since analysts can see several years of continuing growth. However, as its price-to-earnings ratio continues to expand, the stock becomes increasingly overvalued in relation to those earnings. It becomes similar to the prospective doughnut shop buyer becoming so enthusiastic about buying the shop that he or she agrees to a price that's twenty-five times its current profits. If profits stay the same, it will take twenty-five years of operating the business for the profits to pay back the purchase price before the buyer can have the profits. *Perhaps* he or she can increase the profits so much that it is not an unreasonable price to pay.

However, the prospective buyer's chances of success are greatly diminished the further out earnings are projected to increase and the more of those earnings he or she pays for in advance. It's one thing to look out five or six years and expect the business to remain prosperous; it is quite another to look out twenty-five years, during which time anything from health problems to changes in the neighborhood could end the shop's prosperity. In the meantime, having paid a very high price, the buyer's odds of finding another buyer to bail him out without a large loss would be slim.

Therefore, once a stock enters a high-risk zone where it's selling at unreasonable multiples of its earnings prospects, an increasing number of savvy investors will begin taking their profits. If that selling increases and the stock tops out, still more investors will take profits, and soon the stock is in a correction.

When the majority of stocks reach levels where they're selling at unreasonable multiples of their earnings prospects, the entire market becomes overvalued and at risk of topping out. We talked earlier of how exciting uptrends in everything, from Barbie Dolls to California real estate, always eventually reach unsustainable valuation levels where profit takers (sellers) overwhelm buyers and the prices collapse of their own excesses.

The following table shows the *over*valuation levels reached in previous bull markets just before they reversed into bear markets, as measured by the price/earnings ratio, price/book value ratio, and price/dividend ratio of the S&P 500.

MARKET TOP	PRICE/EARNINGS RATIO	PRICE/BOOK VALUE RATIO	PRICE/DIVIDEND RATIO	SUBSEQUENT MARKET DECLINE
1961	23	2.1	35	- 27.1%
1966	18	2.1	34	- 25.2%
1968	19	2.2	36	- 35.9%
1972	20	2.3	38	- 45.1%
1987	23	2.5	38	- 36.1%
1990	17	2.6	35	- 21.2%
1998	28	5.8	67	-19.4%
Average	**21**	**2.8**	**35**	**- 30%**

For comparison, the next table shows the *under*valuation levels reached by the time bear markets reached their lows, and the subsequent rallies or bull markets off those lows.

MARKET BOTTOM	PRICE/EARNINGS RATIO	PRICE/BOOK VALUE RATIO	PRICE/DIVIDEND RATIO	SUBSEQUENT MARKET RISE
1962	14	1.7	25	+ 36%
1966	13	1.9	25	+ 26%
1970	13	1.6	22	+ 46%
1974	7	1.0	16	+ 53%
1978	8	1.1	18	+ 22%
1982	7	1.2	15	+ 64%
1988	12	1.9	26	+ 60%
1991	13	2.3	25	+ 40%
Average	**11**	**1.6**	**21**	**+ 43%**

Obviously, the time to buy is when valuations are low, and the time to sell is when valuations are high. However, just as obviously, valuation levels have varied considerably at each market top, and at each bear market low, and so cannot be used by themselves as market timing tools. They can, however, be used as a clear indication of market risk. The market can usually be considered to be entering high-risk territory on a valuation basis once the price/earnings ratio on the S&P 500 rises above 20, its price/book value ratio rises above 2.5, and its price/dividend ratio rises above 35.

However, the market can remain at levels of extreme overvaluation for some time or, as the spike-up market of 1995 through 1998 clearly demonstrated, other conditions can exist that allow the market to go on to even more overvalued levels. For instance, at the end of 1996, the S&P 500 was already selling at a record forty-five times its dividend yield, four times its book value and, at twenty-one times its earnings, it is afterall, in the "danger" zone. Yet the market gained another 57 percent over the next year and a half (mostly during its favorable seasonal periods).

So, we must also look at other conditions that exist at the time, which might allow valuation levels to move even higher into the danger zone before the market tops out.

INFLATION AND MONETARY CONDITIONS

Without getting too entangled in the mists of economics, declining inflation allows consumers to buy more products per dollar of income, while corporations see their cost of materials and supplies decline, which improves their profit margins. In the same manner, declining interest rates are beneficial to corporate sales and earnings growth because consumers can buy more products and services on credit for the same monthly payments, and corporations can borrow to handle those growing sales at lower cost. In addition, declining interest rates make savings accounts, CDs, money market accounts, and bonds less attractive to investors, which also prompts investors to stick with the stock market longer.

The period from 1996, when the market was already well into the danger zone on a valuation basis, through its significant further rise to early 1998, is a perfect example. Inflation declined throughout the period, falling from an already low 3.5 percent in 1996, as measured by the Consumer Price Index, to 1.8 percent in early 1998, its lowest level since Eisenhower was president. Interest rates also declined sharply during the period, the yield on the thirty-year Treasury bond falling from 7.2 to 5.9 percent, its lowest level in thirty years.

Those unusual declines in both inflation and interest rates allowed both the strong economy, which had already remained in an uptrend for an unusually long time, and corporate earnings growth to continue, and provided an environment that convinced investors to stick with the stock market even though valuation levels were already extremely high.

So, at the same time that we watch for valuation levels to climb into the danger zone, we must adjust our concern over the risk through observation of the direction of inflation and interest rates.

INVESTOR SENTIMENT

Another important measurement of the risk level as each unfavorable seasonal period approaches is the level of optimism or pessimism being exhibited by investors and investment advisors at the time.

We've already learned that strong uptrends cause participants to increasingly ignore risk and become euphorically convinced that rising prices will continue forever, and that their optimism reaches an extreme at market tops. We also know that as serious bear markets get underway, investor sentiment becomes increasingly pessimistic, with the pessimism reaching an extreme at bear market lows. We're concerned only with whether investor sentiment is at an extreme of optimism as a seasonally unfavorable period approaches.

The degree of public participation in the market at any time is one measurement used by market professionals. A healthy percentage of public investors are interested and participate in the market throughout their lives. However, to the rest of the public, and even the media, the stock market is a boring game that's played in New York, and they have no interest until a bull market becomes unusually exciting and big profits have already been made. They then want into the game and, in an effort to catch up to the big gains they've been hearing about, become increasingly unrestrained in their enthusiasm and willingness to pay any price for the stocks they buy to enter the game. It's always this late, unrestrained public buying that drives bull markets to unreasonable levels of valuation. So, market professionals watch statistics of public participation as one sign of changing risk. That indication of market risk is as old as the market itself.

In his memoirs, Jesse Livermore, the famed stock market operator of the early 1900s, spoke of his early success on Wall Street, when after studying market patterns as a clerk at a regional brokerage firm, and running a borrowed $5 into several thousand dollars, he moved to New York to become a full-time trader. Livermore said, "I almost immediately ran into a bull market, and over the next year or two my small stake grew to $50,000 [a huge sum in 1900 dollars]. "But then the public finally got wind of it [the bull market] and went stock mad. I knew the end was near."

Livermore was right. Several months later, on May 9, 1901, the stock market collapsed so fast that of the experience, Livermore said:

> The price collapses were just awful. The trading floor was way behind the sell orders, and the tape was running so far behind the transactions, that a seller had no way of knowing at what price he was selling. A stock that closed at $100 the night before, opened at $80 the next morning. If an investor then put in an order to sell, by the time the order reached the trading floor and worked its way through the backlog, the price was $60. A 40 percent loss in hours.

Among the measurements modern-day professionals use to gauge public enthusiasm:

- The amount of new money flowing into mutual funds
- The ease with which stock promoters are finding buyers for stocks of unknown new companies they bring to market in IPOs (initial public offerings)
- The percentage of U.S. household assets that have moved into the stock market
- Anecdotal evidence, including growth or decline of employment in the brokerage industry, the growth of new mutual funds initiated to meet investor demand, the growth or decline in the number of investment clubs, the level of interest in speculative stocks, and the degree of interest in the stock market by the general (nonfinancial) media

Once again, none of these have definite limits at which they signal a market top. They provide us only with a gut feeling of the risk, indicated by the general public's subdued or extreme interest in the market.

REAL MEASUREMENTS

Actual measurements of investor optimism or pessimism can be found in the work of those who compile statistics based on polling specific groups of market participants.

The best known and most widely followed is probably *Investors Intelligence* in New Rochelle, New York. This firm has been tracking the sentiment of investment advisory newsletters since 1948. It releases its findings weekly, providing the percentage of investment letters that are currently bullish, bearish, or neutral on the market.

The *American Association of Individual Investors*, in Chicago, polls its national members and reports weekly on the percentage that are bullish, bearish, or neutral on the market.

Consensus Inc., Kansas City, Missouri, polls and reports the sentiment of most major professional brokers and money managers.

Market Vane, Pasadena, California, reports bullish, bearish, and neutral percentages of futures traders.

The current sentiment of each group can be obtained on a continuous basis directly from the firms at reasonable subscription costs, or for our limited need of once a year, can be obtained from *Barron's,* which is available at newsstands.

The interesting thing is that, though individually they may have impressive performance records, taken as a group, each group—whether individual investors, professional brokers, money managers, investment newsletters, or futures traders—has the same "crowd psychology." They become, as a group, overly optimistic by the time the market reaches a top, and overly pessimistic by the time the market reaches an important correction low.

The percentage of bullishness or bearishness of these various groups is meaningless most of the time since the numbers meander up and down, or are trending in one direction or the other. But when they reach extremes, they do have meaning and are used as a "contrary" indicator by professionals. That is, by the time "the crowd" becomes too optimistic, too enthusiastic, it's usually a sign the market has reached an intermediate-term peak, and a correction will follow. In the other direction, in a market decline, by the time the crowd's pessimism or bearishness has reached an extreme reading, it's a sign the market is near the end of the correction.

Investors sometimes have trouble getting their mind around that scenario, and the situation does require some thought. One would think that if everyone has become extremely optimistic about the market, it would increase the level of buying and the market would go even higher. One would think that in a bear market if everyone has become extremely pessimistic about the market, it would increase the amount of selling and the market would go even lower. However, the situation is that by the time optimism in a bull market reaches an extreme, everyone with any inclination to be in the market is already fully invested, so the market has run out of fuel to drive it higher. At that point, it takes very little profit taking for selling pressure to take over. Similarly, in a bear market, by the time pessimism reaches an extreme, everyone who is inclined to sell has pretty much done so. At that point, it takes very little buying by bargain hunters to reverse the market to the upside.

On the *Investors Intelligence* numbers, the market is at high risk of a correction when the bullish percentage reaches 52 to 56 percent, and the bearish percentage drops below 23 percent. In the other direction, begin looking for a correction low when the bearish percentage reaches 55 to 62 percent, and the bullish percentage drops below 23 percent.

With the other services, the numbers tend to become even more lopsided, with the percentage of bulls getting as high as 70 percent at market tops, and as low as 20 percent at correction bottoms.

As with valuation levels, inflation rates, interest rates, and economic conditions, the sentiment readings can't be used by themselves as a buy or sell signal on the market. The crowd can always become even more optimistic at various market tops, or more pessimistic at bear market lows, depending on other conditions that are in place at the time.

OVERBOUGHT OR OVERSOLD?

Finally, we need to look to our technical charts of the market. We want to know if the market is overbought, or likely to be overbought by the time the unfavorable period begins. *Barron's Dictionary of Finance and Investment Terms* defines overbought as the "description of a security or a market that has recently experienced a significant price rise and is therefore vulnerable to a price drop (called a correction by technical analysts). When a stock has been overbought, there are fewer buyers left to drive the price up further."

Analysts use various charting techniques to measure whether a stock or a market is overbought. One of the simplest is shown in the following chart.

We simply overlay its 200-day moving average (m.a.) over a chart of the S&P 500, a simple procedure in all stock market software. Note that its 200-day moving average tends to be an

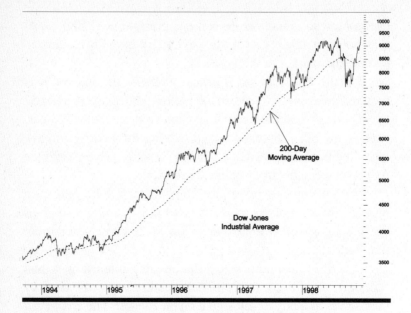

equilibrium level for the market. When the market rises too far, or for too long a time, above its 200-day moving average, the moving average acts as a magnet and pulls the market back to it. When the market declines below the moving average, the moving average draws it back up.

It can also be noted that even in as powerful a bull market as was seen from 1995 through 1998, the 200-day moving average pulled the market down to it at least once each year, in what were 10 to 13 percent "corrections." Remember why they are called corrections? Because they "correct" the overbought conditions (and at least partially correct the overvaluation conditions).

When the market declines to its 200-day m.a., and then resumes its uptrend, it is said to have found "support" at its 200-day m.a., a sign of a continuing bull market.

Just as the 200-day m.a. tends to act as support for minor corrections in bull markets, so the 200-day m.a. tends to act as overhead "resistance" in bear markets. That is, market rallies within ongoing bear markets tend to run out of steam as soon as the market climbs back up to the vicinity of its 200-day m.a.

By simply observing the degree to which the S&P 500 has become extended above or below its 200-day moving average, we can get a feel for whether the market is overbought or oversold, and by observing the seasons, we can recognize whether the odds favor a decline that will at least pull the market down to its 200-day m.a.

The next chart adds an overbought–oversold oscillator that actually measures overbought and oversold conditions.

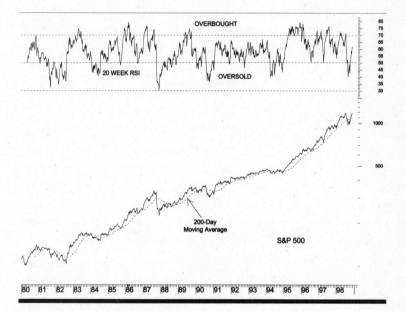

In this chart, we've moved out in time to show nineteen years of market activity. Therefore, it's not as easy to see the support usually provided by the 200-day moving average. However, it allows us to see how the 20-week RSI (Relative Strength Index) is used to confirm what the 200-day m.a. is telling us about whether the market is in overbought territory. This indicator is provided in all basic market charting software, along with a number of similar overbought–oversold oscillators that can be used to provide similar confirmation of overbought and oversold conditions. It can be seen that in 1987 and 1990, as the most recent bear markets approached, the market first became significantly overbought.

A MORE REPRESENTATIVE CHART

Unfortunately for demonstration purposes, the most recent bear markets were the briefest bear markets in history and were followed by the longest period in history without a bear market. I've included a chart of the market activity from 1970 to 1982, a period of more normal market volatility. It will better demonstrate what we're doing and will illustrate more typical bear markets than the brief events of 1987 and 1990.

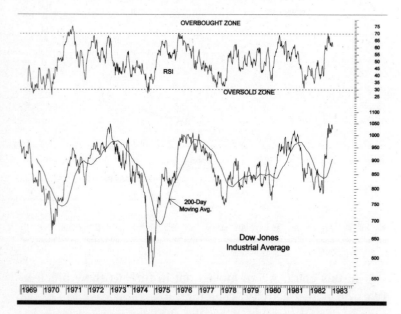

Note again the ability of the market to rise only so far above its 200-day m.a. before becoming so "overbought" that a correction at least to the moving average becomes inevitable. Note also how, unlike in the unusual market of the late 1990s, the RSI indicator remains in overbought territory only briefly before the market normally tops out. The chart also shows how, when the market is in a downtrend, or bear market, the 200-day m.a. becomes overhead resistance in most rally attempts.

Finally, and possibly most important for 1990's investors, note how long bear markets usually last once they get underway. As mentioned before, the brief bear markets of 1987 and 1990, which lasted just a couple of months, were aberrations, the shortest bear markets in history. Unfortunately, that situation, followed by the longest period in history, nine years, without *any* bear markets, has left the majority of investors woefully unprepared in their expectations of what the next bear market will look like.

PICKING OUR TARGET STOCKS TO SELL SHORT

Assuming that we have taken our profits from a seasonally positive period, and have entered a seasonally unfavorable period, with the market overvalued, overbought, and investor optimism at an extreme, our next step is to select our target stocks and sell them short.

We know that in a declining market, the downdraft will carry 75 percent of stocks with it, so even based on throwing darts at the stock listings, the odds are in our favor. However, we can improve our odds significantly by employing just a couple of tools.

INSIDER SELLING

We've already learned that corporate insiders have a history of trading in and out of their company's stock with such excellent timing that it causes market professionals to watch insider activity closely, as a guide to their own investments. Obviously, corporate insiders, that is, a corporation's top management, board of directors, and largest investors, will always know more about what's going on at a company, and what its future prospects are, than any outsider. For instance, they will always be the first to know if sales or earnings have begun to stall, or if a new product from R&D is not working as well as expected, or if negotiations on a pending acquisition are looking less promising. Even professional analysts can only know what management is willing to tell them at the time about future prospects.

We can use the same insider information the professionals employ to compile our initial list of potential short sale candidates. The SEC requires that all corporate insiders report the sales and purchases of their company's stock in a timely manner, and it is public information. The data is available to anyone directly from the SEC. However, with 7300 stocks trading just on the NYSE and NASDAQ, and dozens, even hundreds, of insiders at each company, the data is voluminous. It's also very confusing in its raw form since many different types of filings are required.

Fortunately, a number of reliable sources collect and sort the data into usable information. *The Insiders*, Deerfield Beach, Florida, at $100 per year, is one of the lowest cost and gets the job done sufficiently for our purpose. Companies where insider buying or selling is measurable are listed alphabetically, along with the number of buyers and sellers over the last twelve months. Included is a proprietary ranking from 0 to 10, based on the significance of the activity, 0 indicating the most significant selling, and 10 the most significant buying.

We will first narrow our search for short sale candidates by compiling a list of those companies that have high levels of insider selling. Then we will look at the charts of those companies, looking for those where momentum appears to have reversed to the downside in a meaningful way.

To spot a momentum reversal, we'll use a momentum indicator similar to the MACD indicator we used on the Dow to more accurately pinpoint the entries and exits of our Seasonal Timing System, but altered to provide intermediate-term buy and sell signals.

Following are a few examples of short sale recommendations we made to our subscribers during the market's unfavorable period in 1998, and our analysis of each.

The first is BankBoston. We did not get to this stock until July 1998. This is what the chart told us at the time.

BankBoston stock had been overbought in April on the Relative Strength Index, but the buying pressure was already receding, as indicated by relative strength coming down from overbought territory. The MACD momentum indicator had triggered a sell signal in May, after which the stock moved sideways for a couple of months, tried to rally again, but failed at its previous high, creating a "double top." The Relative Strength Index also failed to move back to its old high, rolling over to the downside again, and the MACD had just broken down further (in July). We immediately checked the insider activity at BankBoston, and learned that only one insider had bought more shares in recent months, whereas thirteen had sold. We then checked its price/earnings ratio and discovered BankBoston was selling at seventeen times its estimated year-ahead earnings, considerably higher than its historical average of around 11.

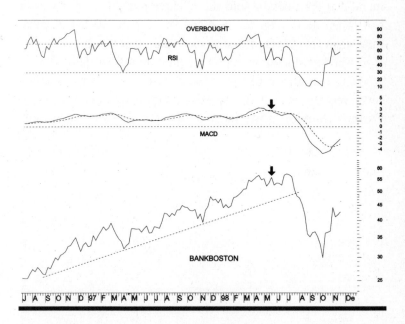

With technical conditions confirmed as bearish, we searched for fundamental conditions that might explain the situation. We searched through recent headlines and stories about BankBoston by going to several Internet sites, including our own, that allow free perusal of several months of historical Dow Jones headlines. From those stories, we learned that much of the recent strength in the stock was due to the takeover activity in the banking industry and hope among investors that BankBoston might receive a takeover offer. In other words, the recent strength wasn't due to improved earnings prospects or anything BankBoston itself had accomplished. We also discovered that BankBoston was in the midst of a major expansion into Latin America countries and that international operations already accounted for 31 percent of its business. That information set off an alarm bell in our mind since we had just been reading about how the Asian currency and economic crises seemed to be spreading to Latin America. That was all the information we needed to create an expectation that BankBoston shares were headed lower, and we should immediately recommend that the stock be sold short. Three months later, the stock had fallen more than $25 a share, or 45 percent. It had taken more than two years for the stock to gain that much.

Another stock that met our requirements was Chrysler.

Chrysler shares had been bid up almost 100 percent in just seven months on excitement over the company's pending merger with Daimler Benz, the manufacturer of Mercedes Benz

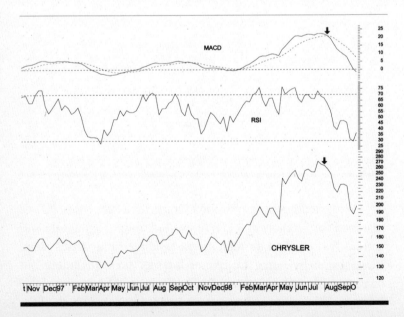

automobiles. However, the insiders at Chrysler didn't seem to share the public's enthusiasm. There had been no insider buying since the merger had been announced, but thirty-two insiders had sold. In the meantime, the share price was in overbought territory with relative strength weakening, and the MACD had just triggered a sell signal.

Searching for a plausible reason why insiders were not sharing the public's enthusiasm, we learned from historical *Dow Jones News/Retrieval* items that some analysts were concerned the giant merger would create an unwieldy monster. Others felt the wide cultural differences between the brash, aggressive American approach to management, and the conservative, somber German approach at Daimler Benz, would create serious problems and conflicts, and prevent the merger from going smoothly. At the same, the merger was taking place amid worldwide overcapacity in the auto industry.

Our search criteria were met, and we recommended the short sale of Chrysler. The share price fell 30 percent from peak to trough.

You need to realize that the search takes some work. Probably twenty or thirty candidates fall by the wayside, for one reason or another, for every one that meets all the criteria even though we begin with a candidate list consisting only of companies with heavy insider selling.

Disney was another stock that showed up as selling at a very high multiple of earnings, with heavy insider selling, and triggered a sell signal on technical indicators just as 1998's unfavorable period approached. A search of recent *Dow Jones News/Retrieval* items revealed that earnings estimates were being lowered by analysts on concerns that international economic plunges would affect foreign revenues from Disney movies, and that its new Animal Kingdom theme park in Florida might take attendance away from the company's existing nearby theme parks. The stock plunged 45 percent from its May peak to its October low.

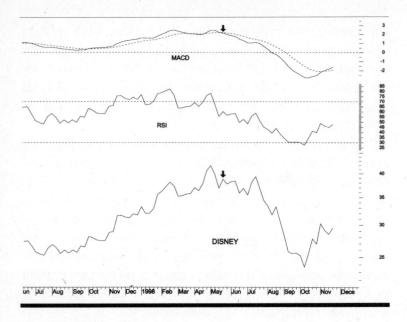

DIVERSIFY

Keep in mind that just as you would not buy only one stock in a bull market, it's important to diversify with a number of short sales for the downside. Just like in a bull market, not all picks are going to be winners.

Additionally, whether you are selling short in anticipation of a decline in a stock's price or buying (long) in anticipation of a rise in a stock's price, you must engage in some form of portfolio management. If you're not willing to do that, you should not be dabbling in the stock market in the first place. It's no place to be careless. One of the most important obligations of that management, right up there with diversification, is limiting losses.

The most successful investors in the world, from Peter Lynch to George Soros, will freely admit they are wrong 30 percent of the time. Their success comes from cutting their losses quickly when they're wrong, while allowing the profits to run on their right decisions. You cannot become immovably convinced of the correctness of your decision either to buy a stock *or* to sell it short, and simply hold on regardless, waiting for the market to eventually prove that you were right. That's known as falling in love with your stocks (being unwilling to part with them no matter how badly they treat you). You *will* make mistakes, probably at least 30 percent of the time in normal market conditions. However, that's true in both bull and bear markets, in buying long and selling short. It is not an extra hazard confined to short selling.

There's only one indication that a mistake has been made. The stock will move in the wrong direction. *Don't ignore it.* You must make yourself realize that a stock that moves 10 percent in the wrong direction is warning you to revisit the reasons you made your decision to buy it, or sell it short, in the first place. If those reasons are no longer valid or something has changed, the warning of the 10 percent move of the stock in the wrong direction gives you a first opportunity to bail out with minimum damage. If a stock moves 15 percent in the wrong direction, it's clearly telling you that you made a mistake. Cut the loss before it grows worse. Let the profits on the other 70 percent of your correct decisions run. You'll be taking a giant step toward joining the ranks of successful investors, and leave behind those who watch their mistakes go down, waiting for them to come back "so they won't lose so much."

WATCH WHERE YOU ARE IN THE UNFAVORABLE SEASON

Another piece of advice I have learned the hard way is to be careful initiating short sales too close to the end of an unfavorable period. You might not be allowing the stock enough time to perform for you if the next favorable seasonal period arrives early.

DETAILS OF THE SHORT SELLING PROCESS

- An investor must establish a "margin account," or change his cash account to a margin account, in order to sell stocks short.

- Generally speaking, stocks can be sold short only "on an uptick." That is, if a stock is falling sharply, with each successive sale at a lower price than the previous sale, an order to sell the stock short cannot be executed until there is first a transaction at a higher price than the previous sale.

    For instance, suppose you place an order to sell 100 shares of XYZ short, with the last trade having taken place at $90. If XYZ shares are declining when your sell order hits the trading floor, and transactions on XYZ take place at 89¾, 89½, 89¼, 89, 88½, 87¾, 86¾, and then 87, your order to sell short will not take place until that uptick from 86¾ to 87 even though you placed your order when the stock was at 90 and all the normal sell orders came in *after* yours. The purpose of the rule is so that in a sharp market decline, short sellers cannot come in and accelerate the decline by continuous selling of stocks they don't own.

    Therefore, it's usually difficult, and inadvisable, to make a short sale on a day when the stock is plunging, since there may be few, if any, trades that take place on an uptick. The uptick rule also makes it strongly advisable to place "limit orders," rather than "at the market orders." That way, you are specifying the lowest price at which you are willing to take a short position in the stock, and an unexpected plunge in the stock, combined with the uptick rule, will not have you selling short at a much lower price than you expected to receive.

- It's very dangerous to sell short the stock of small companies, particularly low-priced stocks with a relatively small number of shares trading. Even if you're right in expecting the stock should move lower, it's relatively easy for the company or a large holder of the stock to halt the stock's decline, and reverse the price sharply to the upside. For instance, suppose a small stock that is selling at $10 a share, and normally trades 5000 shares a day, declines to $7 with the company believing that it's short selling that's causing the decline. It would cost them only $35,000 a day for a few days to double the number of shares trading and probably drive the price back up to $10 or more, forcing short sellers to close out their positions with losses.

A CAUTION REGARDING INSIDER ACTIVITY

Not all insider selling reflects the insiders' expectations for the company's stock. A vice president might simply need to raise cash for a new house or a divorce. Management may be receiving part of their pay in the form of stock and need to sell some periodically to turn it into income. At Microsoft, and other high-tech companies where insiders have become extremely wealthy, but all of their wealth is tied up in company stock, insiders have to sell stock on a regular basis in order to have the use of their wealth.

CONCLUSION

We can make significant gains in a bear market, or even in meaningful corrections back to support levels, gains that will nicely enhance the gains we keep from the favorable seasonal periods. To do so, we need to first determine that market risk is high as an unfavorable period approaches, based on valuation levels, overbought–oversold conditions, and investor sentiment. We then need to zero in on specific stocks that have exceptional promise as short sale candidates by looking for those that are very overbought on the charts, where insiders are selling, where momentum has just topped out and rolled over to the downside (a sell signal on the technical indicators), and where fundamental reasons in the company's situation support the expectation that the stock price will now head lower.

In the next chapter, we will explore how we can take similar advantage of falling prices while limiting our risk to a predetermined amount of money.

CHAPTER 10

LIMIT RISK AND GAIN LEVERAGE—WITH OPTIONS

Let's assume that its mid-April and the unfavorable seasonal period is about to begin. IBM is selling at $135 a share, and my analysis and the charts are telling me it should soon decline 35 percent to get back to its fair value. I could sell short 100 shares of IBM, with the goal of making some portion of that 35 percent, and would have a $13,500 short position in the trade.

An alternative would be to buy put options on IBM, which would cost considerably less, yet would have the potential to make almost as large a profit on a dollar basis, and a much larger profit in terms of return on investment.

A put option is an option, or right, to sell a stock at a specified price at any time during a specified period. In the example given, it's April, and IBM is trading at 135. An IBM June 125 put option would allow me to sell IBM for $125 a share, any time prior to the options expiration date in June, *regardless of the price IBM is trading at when I decide to exercise the option.* That may sound strange, but yes, buying the June 125 put allows me to sell 100 shares of IBM at $125 even if IBM has plunged to $75 at the time. Such an option contract would cost in the vicinity of $550. If I am right that IBM is going to go down, and it declines 35 percent to $88 a share before the option's expiration date in mid-June, I can buy 100 shares of

IBM for $8800 and immediately sell them for $12,500 via the put option, and pocket roughly a $3700 profit. (In reality, it isn't even that much effort since the put options themselves would simply be sold for the same profit.)

Note that if I had instead sold 100 shares of IBM short for $13,500 and it had declined to the same point, where I could close out the position by buying 100 shares for $8800, I would have made a $4700 profit, or 53 percent, on the trade.

However, by investing only $550 in the put options and making $3700 on the trade, I made a 670 percent profit on my investment.

Of equal importance, by going the option route, I limited my risk to a predetermined amount. If I was wrong, and *never* came to admit it, allowing the option to expire worthless in June, I still could not lose more than $550 on the trade. However, if I had sold short 100 shares of IBM at $135, for a total position of $13,500, and had been wrong, even if I closed out the position as soon as it moved 10 percent against me, I would still have had a $1350 loss. If I hung on until the position moved 15 percent against me before closing the position, I'd have had a $2025 loss.

Whoa! 670 percent profit versus 53 percent, on the same trade, and with less risk? What's the catch?

The catch is that if I simply sell IBM short, and I'm right in my expectation that it has seen its high and will decline significantly, but it takes longer than I expect for the decline to take place, I will still make my profit. However, in buying the IBM June 125 put options, I have to be right not only on IBM's direction, but also on the time frame. If IBM moves only sideways or down slightly by June so that it is still trading above $125, the options are still going to expire worthless, even if IBM subsequently plunges 50 percent in July or August.

However, the use of options rather than selling short should certainly be considered. It has a number of advantages.

For instance, though everyone feels comfortable being 100 percent invested during bull markets, *no one* is going to feel comfortable being 100 percent short in a bear market. It's just the nature of the beast. Bull markets last longer, and so our experience is related more to holding long positions. Bull markets are nice things. They make everyone happy and confident. The gains are easy to understand. Bear markets produce gloom and fear. No one knows what's going on. Why are stocks of good companies falling apart? Everyone you meet is losing money. The losses are not slow and steady as the gains were in the bull market. The declines are swift and brutal. So even when *you* are making gains in a bear market, you're doing so in an atmosphere of gloom and doom, and can easily be intimidated by it.

Options allow you to leave most of your portfolio in cash, safely earning interest during a severe correction or bear market, while you put only a small portion of your assets at risk. Yet, thanks to the high leverage of options, your gains can be comparable to having your whole portfolio at work in the market.

For example, suppose you place 95 percent of your portfolio in cash, safely earning 5 percent interest, as an unfavorable seasonal period begins, and use just 5 percent of your portfolio to go after gains from the expected bear market, through the use of put options rather than short sales. If you totally misread every chart and piece of information you look at, are totally wrong on market direction, totally wrong on the direction of every stock you select, and totally fail to cut losses on any positions when an error becomes obvious, and so let every option position expire worthless, the total "drawdown" on your overall portfolio would still be only 5 percent. You *can't* lose more than the entire 5 percent you put at risk. And the 5 percent annual interest the other 95 percent of your portfolio is earning will even offset some of that.

Yet, if you have been careful to run a number of positions at all times so that your eggs are not all in one basket, faithfully follow a procedure of cutting losses on positions that move against you, and have decent ability in making the initial selections, it would not be at all unusual to have that 5 percent of your portfolio triple in a correction, or grow tenfold in a serious market decline. The result is that 5 percent of your portfolio in put options can produce as large a gain for your overall portfolio as would be achieved by having 100 percent of your portfolio at risk in short sales.

Of course, the secret is the leverage afforded by options. A 10 percent move in a $100 stock can easily triple the value of an option on the stock. No wonder then that the trading volume of options has exploded upward since they were introduced.

ARE THEY NUTS?

Why would someone sell you the right to "put IBM stock to him or her" at a price of $125 a share, when it might be worth only $75 at the time? We have to realize that for everyone who thinks a stock is going to go down, there has to be someone who thinks it's going to go up, and vice versa, or there could be no market.

The seller of a put option usually wants to own IBM, but would like to own it at a lower price than it's currently trading at, if possible. So, with IBM trading at $135 a share, the seller reasons that if he or she sells a two-month IBM 125 put option for 5½, and IBM stays above 125, he or she will just pocket the $5.50 per share without having made any investment. However, if IBM declines below 125 and someone puts the stock to the option seller at 125, he or she will be buying IBM at 125 instead of its current price of 135, and will have pocketed the option price of $5.50 per share besides. The option seller figures he or she can't lose.

When IBM instead declines to 75, the option seller still has to buy the shares at $125, and may hold onto them a long time before his or her faith in IBM pays off. Let's hope that does not happen to the seller too often. In any event, with most investors always convinced that prices will move only up, there is never a shortage of those willing to sell put options.

CAUTIONS

A few warnings about the use of options.

If you suffer from poor stock-picking ability or poor investment habits, they will only be magnified when using options. The prices of stock options are far more volatile than the prices of their underlying stocks. That is where the leverage comes from. But keep in mind that leverage is a two-edged sword. When you are right, a 10 percent move in a stock can translate to a 300 percent gain in an option. However, when you are wrong, a 5 percent move in a stock can translate to a 50 percent *loss* on an option.

Strangely, more danger comes from being right too often than from being wrong. Being wrong a normal percentage of the time is going to keep your expectations within reasonable limits and keep you following a discipline. However, you can readily imagine that if you put 2 percent of your portfolio in each of three different option positions, and all three triple in a month, you are going to be sorely tempted to put 5 percent in each of your next three positions, and if those also all triple, the sky becomes the limit. The law of averages, however, has not been repealed. About the time you decide to "go for broke," that is just where you will wind up.

Sticking with a game plan is far more important when you are dealing with leveraged positions. Wisdom gathered from dozens of the famous traders who have become obscenely wealthy trading futures positions is revealing. They all warn that the most difficult but important rule they follow is to never have more than 1/2 to 1 percent of their assets in any one leveraged position.

Realize also that, much more so than when dealing with the stock itself, when using options on a stock, it's important to wait for the expected move to begin before taking the position. When you buy an option, the clock begins running immediately. You can't afford to buy an option on a stock you expect will move *some time*. On the other hand, if you have the common tendency to wait *too* long after making a decision on a stock to see if you were right before committing to it, think twice before considering options. Because they are leveraged moves, letting too much of the stock's expected move slide by before committing will have you paying a much higher price for the option, significantly reducing the potential gain and raising the risk if the stock's move stalls.

A complete guide to options trading is beyond the scope of this book, but numerous books on the subject are available.

Just keep the goal in mind, which is to simply use options rather than short sales for "directional trades" on stocks in a bear market. Don't get bogged down in complex strategies based on options pricing theories as used by options traders who try to take advantage of anomalies in option premiums. You don't need to know about bull spreads, bear spreads, box spreads, calendar spreads, or straddles to simply buy a somewhat out of-the-money, two- or three-month put option for a directional trade on a stock you expect to decline in price in the next couple of months.

CHAPTER 11

THE NEXT BEAR IS GROWLING

History, as well as current economic and market conditions, says odds are high a bear market will be underway in 1999, or by the year 2000 at the latest.

We know what *causes* bear markets. Excesses. Excesses that get so out of control they can be cured only by a serious market correction that carries stock prices considerably lower, correcting their overvaluation levels, correcting investors' over-commitment of assets to the market, correcting the dominance of the stock market in the economy.

The problem for the market as it entered 1999 is that it did so with excesses that are at all-time records in most areas. If we were looking at a sporting event, and some say we are, we'd have to say world-class excesses.

PUBLIC PARTICIPATION

We learned earlier that since stocks first began trading 200 years ago, Wall Street professionals and insiders have used the degree of public participation and investor enthusiasm as a gauge of whether the market was nearing a major top.

As the market entered 1999, public enthusiasm for stocks was not simply at *high* levels; it was at mania levels.

The first chart shows how money has been poured into mutual funds since the brief 1987 and 1990 bear markets.

Assets of Mutual Funds (in billions)

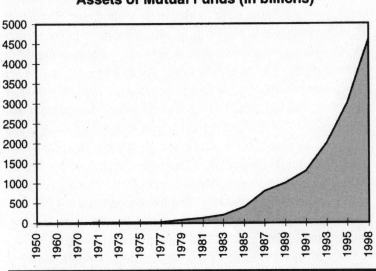

The next chart shows the number of new individual mutual fund accounts that have been set up just in the last few years of market euphoria.

Number of Mutual Fund Shareholder Accounts (millions)

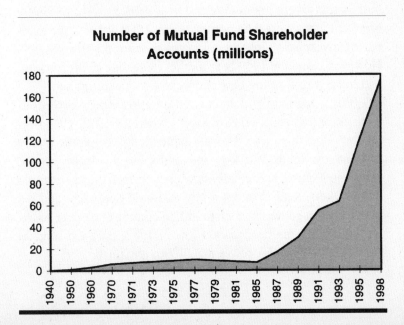

What do the charts tell us? That the total amount of money in mutual funds has surged to almost $5 trillion, and 85 percent of all that money was placed there only since the 1990 bear market. For instance, just $45 billion flowed into mutual funds in 1990, and only $85 billion in 1994. But in 1996, the inflow set an all-time record of $324 billion, and went on to still another record of $378 billion in 1997. Although inflow slowed from that record pace in 1998, the total amount of money in mutual funds continued to soar. The second chart shows that the number of individual mutual fund accounts has also spiked up, from just 20 million in 1987 to almost 180 million in 1998. That represents a good portion of the population that has become interested in the stock market only in the last few years, during the most exciting, unsustainable, final phase a bull market has ever seen.

As further evidence of the unprecedented public interest, the following chart shows the number of small investment clubs that have operated through the years, as individual investors gather in small local groups to study stocks and pool resources for investments.

Note the surge in new investment clubs in the 1960s when bull markets were impressive and bear markets were relatively brief and less severe than normal. From 1960 to 1969, the number of investment clubs almost tripled, from 5500 to 14,000. However, came the 1969 bear market (a decline of 36 percent), and interest in forming new clubs came to an abrupt halt.

When the market then entered a period when corrections were more frequent, and particularly when the 1973–1974 bear market (a decline of 45 percent) came along, the public totally lost interest in the market, and clubs began closing down. Investment clubs, particularly new ones formed during exciting bull markets, tend to adopt a buy and hold approach, and it's not much fun gathering each month to commiserate over growing *losses*. By the bear market low in 1982, only the original core number of clubs, fewer than 4000, remained.

Growth of Investment Clubs

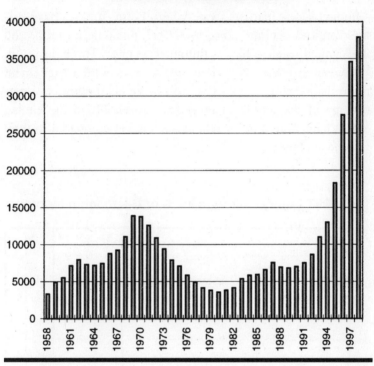

Interest in the market remained subdued long after the new bull market began in 1982, when the Dow was at 780. As the chart clearly shows, interest did not pick up to a significant degree until 1993 (by which time the Dow had already more than quadrupled to 3400). But by far the greatest interest in forming new clubs began in 1996, after the Dow had already soared to 5500, 700 percent higher than its level in 1982.

The excitement since has been eye-popping. It's hard to believe, but beginning in 1995, an average of 550 new investment clubs have formed every month; *that's eighteen per day.* By January 1999, some 38,000 small investment clubs were operating in the United States. Excessive market excitement?

WORLD-CLASS ENTHUSIASM

Although stock markets from Asia to Latin America have suffered serious declines since mid-1997, markets in Europe and the United States have continued strong. Through it all, European investors have been able to control their excitement more than U.S. investors. The following chart shows the percentage of disposable income that households in the United States have committed to the stock market compared to their European counterparts.

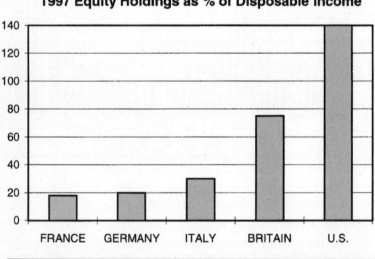

1997 Equity Holdings as % of Disposable Income

How have U.S. investors managed to place more than 100 percent of their disposable income in the stock market? By means of an activity for which Americans are famous.

PLAY NOW, PAY LATER

Another method of measuring excessive investor participation is the degree to which investors have run out of cash and gone on to *borrow* additional money for the market. One such measurement is the level of margin debt. Buying stocks on margin consists of putting up 50 percent of the purchase price of a stock in cash, and borrowing the rest from the brokerage firm that handles the transaction.

The beauty of it is that if you have $100,000 and buy on margin, you can buy $200,000 worth of stocks (or mutual funds). If those stocks go up 25 percent, you have yourself a tidy $50,000 profit. Since you put up only $100,000 of your own money, you don't have a 25 percent profit, but a 50 percent profit, on your investment. Leverage your stock market gains that way a few times, and you're looking at a substantial march toward riches. *If you always make gains.*

The problem, of course, is that should your $200,000 worth of stock bought on margin decline by 30 percent, you've lost $60,000. Since you invested only $100,000 of your own money, that's a 60 percent loss, and you have only $40,000 left. Should the stock decline 50 percent, you have nothing left.

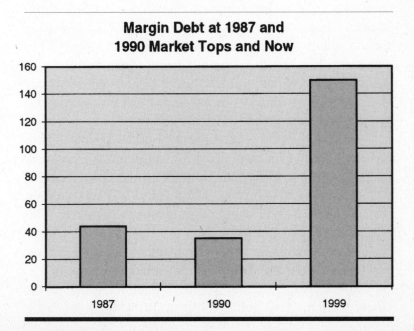

**Margin Debt at 1987 and
1990 Market Tops and Now**

But, I digress. Obviously, the degree to which investors are willing to buy stocks on margin will reveal their level of excitement and euphoria regarding the market at any particular time.

As this chart on the previous page shows, total margin debt climbed to $44 billion in the excitement leading to the market peak just prior to the 1987 market crash, then plunged during the crash. It climbed back up to $35 billion at the market top just prior to the 1990 bear market and, of course, also plunged during that bear market. The level of margin debt as the market entered 1999? *Would you believe $148 billion?*

In addition, there's considerable anecdotal evidence that investors have been refinancing home mortgages and borrowing against life insurance policies to an unusual degree in the last few years, and that much of that equity in safe, but boring, assets has also been shifted to the stock market. Brokerage firms are even reporting some investors trying to purchase stocks on their credit cards. With credit card interest running as high as 21 percent annually, that's quite a sign of confidence in the market. And it apparently *is* happening. Last October, an investor scam was closed down in Florida, in which the scamsters took investors for an estimated $12 million by promising them a return of 300 percent per year on their money. The shock was not that there are still people who fall for such schemes, but that one man who lost $27,000 said the money was all raised by advances on his credit cards because the rest of his assets were already in the market.

We would expect such excitement and euphoria to have investors' asset allocation decidedly tilted toward the stock market, and the following charts, based on surveys of its members by the American Institute of Individual Investors, confirm that, with allocation to stocks extreme even in relation to 1990 allocation percentages.

Even Congress became overwhelmed with stock market euphoria in 1996 and 1997, and committees were formed to look into investing the nation's Social Security system in the stock market. The public chimed in with enthusiastic

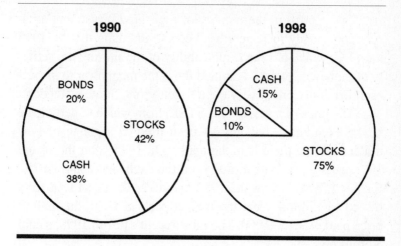

endorsement of the idea. Congress put out charts and statistics, based on the market's unusual rise through the 1990s, showing how much more money would be available to retiree's based on the profits the system would reap from the stock market. Warnings from Fed Chairman Greenspan about the market's inevitable ups and downs, followed by the market correction later in 1998, cooled off Congress's interest in the idea, at least temporarily.

PARTY TIME ON WALL STREET

With their customers insisting on buying Wall Street's products at any price, you would expect excesses to carry over to Wall Street, and the numbers confirm the degree to which the bubbly flows.

The number of registered stock brokers has doubled since 1982, to more than 550,000 in 1998. Their salaries, commission income, and year-end bonuses, many well up in the millions, have been mind boggling. The average broker was paid $175,000 per year in 1998, and that average was dragged down significantly by all the new hires and trainees taken on in 1997 and 1998 to handle the rush.

The growth in the number of registered investment advisors and money managers has been so dramatic that by 1995 the SEC, which has the responsibility of monitoring the activity of money managers, admitted it has the manpower to inspect each firm only once every eight to ten years. Some watchdog.

The price of a seat on the NYSE, from which to participate in the excitement, has always been used as a gauge of how much euphoria there is in the market. In 1975, after the severe 1973–1974 bear market, a seat on the exchange could be had for just $55,000. Near the 1987 market peak, a seat sold for a record $1 million. Near the market peak in 1990, the highest price paid was $500,000. The most recent sale? In 1998, a cool $2 million.

In 1982, there were only 539 mutual funds. There are now more than 7000. In the last few years, new mutual funds have been introduced at the incredible rate of *more than one per day.*

The party on Wall Street seems endless, but participants know it isn't. Wall Street is only too aware of its boom and bust history. The observations that stockbrokers drive BMWs in bull markets and taxicabs in bear markets, while brokerage firm analysts earn million-dollar salaries in bull markets and are unemployed in bear markets, are all too true. It's no wonder Wall Street seems willing to do or say almost anything to keep the money flowing in.

STOCKS TAKING OVER THE ECONOMY?

Economists become concerned when too much of the nation's assets are allocated to stock market risk. One method used is to compare the total value, or capitalization, of all the stocks on the NYSE to the nation's Gross Domestic Product (GDP), which is the aggregate value of all the goods and services produced by the nation's businesses and government.

The upper bars of the preceding chart show the degree to which the total value of stocks on the NYSE approached the value of the nation's Gross Domestic Product at previous major

MARKET CAPITALIZATION AS % OF GDP AT MARKET TOPS

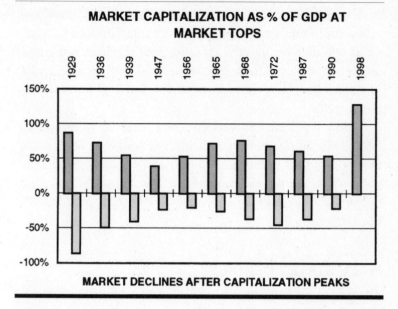

MARKET DECLINES AFTER CAPITALIZATION PEAKS

market tops. For instance, in 1929, stock market capitalization reached an alarming 87 percent of GDP. At the market top in 1936, it reached 73 percent. In 1968, it reached 76 percent, in 1972, it reached 68 percent, and in 1987, it reached 61 percent.

The lower bars in the chart show the severity of market declines that followed the peaks in capitalization. Note that the largest market declines tended to follow those times when the market became most overbought in relation to GDP.

The ominous warning of the picture is that market capitalization in 1995 exceeded GDP for the first time in history, and went on to reach a high of 128 percent of GDP in 1998. Extreme? Mania?

VALUATION LEVELS

In a previous chapter, we looked at how companies are valued based on the multiple at which their stock is selling to the company's earnings, book value, and dividend. We looked at tables that showed that at bear market lows, the stocks that compose the S&P 500 have sold for as little as one times book value, seven times earnings, and eleven times dividend. At previous market tops, the *highest* ratios ever reached, at the most severely overvalued tops, had the S&P 500 selling at 2.5 times its book value, 22.9 times its earnings, and 38.7 times its dividend yield.

How do those numbers compare with recent levels? By late 1998, the S&P 500 was selling at six times book value, thirty-one times earnings, and sixty-nine times its dividend yield. *These are not just somewhat higher valuation ratios, but unbelievably higher than seen at any market peak in at least the last sixty years.*

WALL STREET DENIALS

The only way Wall Street has been able to downplay the valuation risk is with the claim that earnings, book value, and dividend yields don't matter anymore. The most obvious problem with that is that they used the same argument at other market peaks, as well as when the Japanese market reached extreme valuation ratios in 1989. As it turned out in each instance, and will eventually turn out again, earnings, book value, and dividends do matter. They are the only way to cut through the "pay any price to enter the game" euphoria that eventually prevails in bull markets to determine the fundamental value of businesses. The most recent example was the 65 percent plunge back to normal valuation levels by the Japanese market, which began in 1989 and where it remains ten years later.

OVERBOUGHT OR OVERSOLD

Let's look next at whether the market is oversold, as would be expected at a good buying opportunity, or overbought, as would be expected near a market top.

The solid straight line in the following chart is the median trendline for the Dow's rise in this century. As we enter 1999, the

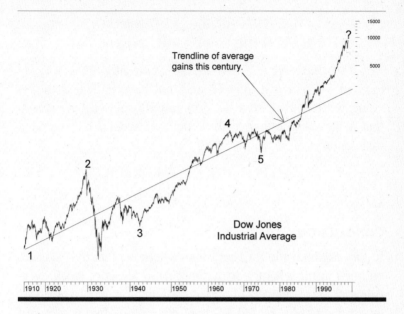

Trendline of average
gains this century.

4

5

Dow Jones
Industrial Average

1

2

3

?

15000

10000

5000

1910 1920   1930   1940   1950   1960   1970   1980   1990

Dow is more overextended above that trendline than it has been since 1929. It would take a plunge of 65 percent for it to correct just back *to* the trendline, which seems inevitable at *some* time. We won't talk about how big a plunge it would take to drop it down to oversold levels below the trendline, yet that is the area where it has tended to trade half the time in this century.

The chart also shows how the market has run in cycles in which a serious bear market comes along an average of every 3.4 years, but also runs in what are known as long-term "secular" moves that encompass several "cyclical" bull and bear markets. The two completed secular bull markets of this century are marked on the chart as 1–2 and 3–4. The long-term secular moves begin with the market oversold to levels well below the median trendline and proceed, even while suffering the fairly frequent cyclical bear markets, until the market is overextended *above* the trendline. Once the subsequent secular bear market begins, it typically does not end until the market is oversold to levels well below the trendline. The gains in the two completed secular bull markets so far this century were:

1–2 (1921–1929)   +597 percent
3–4 (1949–1966)   +611 percent

The third secular bull market, currently underway, is marked 5–? since it may or may not have ended as this is being written. However, we do know its gain so far exceeds that achieved in either of the other two secular bull markets this century:

5–? (1982–1998)   +947 percent

CONCLUSION

It does not take a lot of analysis to determine that the excesses outlined in this chapter, including record levels of stock over-valuation, record levels of public participation, record levels of investor euphoria, record levels of buying on margin, a record percentage of market capitalization related to the nation's Gross Domestic Product, record overbought conditions above the long term trendline, a record length of time without a bear market, and so on, clearly indicate that the market has risen to the highest level of risk it has ever achieved before reversing to the downside of a cycle, and that such a move should be imminent, and is likely to be significant.

CHAPTER 12

HOW SOON?

A WARNING SHOT ACROSS THE BOW

The stock market began 1998 in great style, rallying strongly in the early months during the favorable seasonal period. It was another year starting off with great investor enthusiasm.

In the background, however, ominous events had taken place just over the horizon in the form of severe economic, currency, and market collapses in Asia.

The stock market was not worried since Wall Street was assuring investors, and the media, that the problems in Asia were local events that would not spread outside Asia. They even claimed the Asian collapses would help the U.S. economy and stock market. Their story was that the plunge in Asian currencies, and economic recessions in the region, would result in lower prices for components and supplies purchased by U.S. corporations, which would widen U.S. corporate profit margins.

However, by the spring of 1998, it was obvious that Wall Street's story was flawed. It had ignored the fact that lower-priced Asian products would include lower-priced Asian consumer products, from clothing to automobiles, which would cut into U.S. corporate sales and earnings at home. The rosy scenario also disregarded the effect that recessions in Asia would have on demand for U.S. products being exported to the region. The truth became obvious once major U.S. companies began warning of sales and earnings declines related to Asia, and the U.S. trade gap (imports-exports) began to widen alarmingly.

Wall Street countered the growing concern by pointing out that Asian countries were relatively small trading partners with the United States, and since the problems would not spread beyond Asia, U.S. corporations and the U.S. stock market would not be affected to any meaningful degree.

But then the Russian economy went into a tailspin. The Russian stock market plunged 85 percent. The Russian ruble virtually collapsed.

Next in line, Latin American countries suddenly caught the Asian flu, with currencies, stock markets, and economies, from Brazil and Argentina to Mexico, plunging sharply. Even Canada saw its already weak dollar decline further, to the point that it was worth only sixty-five cents against the U.S. dollar.

The international crises could no longer be shrugged off or explained away by Wall Street. Asia, Latin America, and Canada combined accounted for well over half of U.S. trade.

Increasingly, major U.S. corporations released warnings that forthcoming earnings were being negatively affected, but Wall Street analysts paid little attention, maintaining their earnings estimates for the balance of 1998, and 1999, at very high levels. Federal Reserve Chairman, Alan Greenspan, took note of the anomaly by commenting in congressional testimony that in view of the worsening international crises that were likely to affect the U.S. economy for some time to come, Wall Street's earnings estimates for 1999 were "unrealistic."

Though public investors remained confident, mainly mouthing the assuring words of Wall Street, corporate insiders and Wall Street institutions began selling stocks.

By mid-1998, a decline was underway that soon had the Dow and S&P 500 down 19½ percent, very close to the official 20 percent considered to be the threshold of a bear market. It was the worst correction seen so far in the long bull market from 1990. Most investors are invested in other than the conservative stocks of the Dow and so saw their portfolios down 30 percent and more. Even investors in Warren Buffett's revered holding company, Berkshire Hathaway, saw its stock price decline by 23 percent.

PROFESSIONALS PANIC, PUBLIC INVESTORS HOLD TOUGH

The correction in 1998 was started primarily by profit taking and risk management by Wall Street professionals, institutions, and corporate insiders when the international crises began to threaten the U.S. economy. The media's interpretation was, as one newspaper headline put it, "SMALL INVESTORS HOLD TOUGH AS PROS PANIC!" By and large, public investors did hold tough with their determination to be buy and hold investors, even as Wall Street institutions sold heavily, raising cash. At the subsequent market low, the average buy and hold portfolio was conservatively estimated to be down 25 percent. At that point, Wall Street institutions and insiders began buying back in at the low prices, the next rally was underway, and they made profits from its beginning. Once again, public investors were waiting for their portfolios to "come back."

And still the media did not catch on. After the market's subsequent rally back from the correction lows, the media began pointing out how foolish those who sold had been since the market did come back. They could not seem to fathom that those who sold heavily at the top, sparking the sell-off, were obviously those who bought the bargain prices at the bottom and launched the next rally, and were far better off than those who held through the sell-off.

WAKE-UP CALL

However, public investors, while hanging tough, did get the wake-up call, the realization that the market can go down as well as up. In media interviews near the September low, public investors were expressing thoughts that had not been heard in several years: "I'm getting scared. All my retirement money is in the market," "I might use the next rally to lighten up some." The inflow of new money into mutual funds not only slowed, but actually reversed temporarily to outflow in the month of August, the first outflow on a monthly basis since 1994.

That realization by the public, after eight straight years of one-way market, that the market does go down as well as up raises the odds that at the next rollover to the downside more public investors will participate in the selling.

The normal profile of a bear market is that the first leg down results only in a loss of confidence that the market will always move up. The second leg down consists of an even greater degree of selling due to that loss of confidence. And the third leg down is the panic phase, where the losses become so severe that everyone just wants out regardless of the prices they receive.

The 19½ percent decline in the Dow in 1998 did not quite reach the 20 percent decline that is usually the minimum required to identify a bear market, but it may well have fulfilled the requirement of a first leg down, or warning shot, that will bring more serious selling at the next "scare."

It was interesting that when the market began to rally back strongly in October, it was just what our Seasonal Timing System would have us expect. The market's sharpest decline in the bull market had taken place entirely within the unfavorable seasonal period of 1998. The new rally was getting started as the next favorable seasonal period approached.

As its first wake-up call to investors, the fairly significant correction in 1998 did its job of raising the odds that the next leg down will bring in more public selling and thus be more serious, but *it did absolutely nothing to alleviate the overvalued, overbought, overextended conditions of the market. Nor did it have any effect on the extremes of public participation in the market.*

PILING UP THE NEGATIVES

In the meantime, the ominous international distress is liable to be around for some time. By late 1998, the only attempts to solve the crises had been through the International Monetary Fund (IMF), with far from encouraging results. The IMF spent $140 billion on bailout efforts for Indonesia, South Korea, Thailand, and Russia. The money had simply disappeared down a black hole, and all four countries remained basket cases. In the meantime, Harvard Professor Jeffrey Sachs and others were warning that the IMF's approach is just the opposite of what is needed. The IMF requires countries seeking bailout money to agree to tighten their monetary policies and balance their budgets. Sachs warns such policies could create a "global meltdown" and maintains that what is needed is an *easing* of monetary policies and restructuring of debt.

I mention this controversy not because we need to come down on one side or the other, or come up with a solution, when the greatest minds in the world have been unable to do so, but only as an indication that the international crises that have already been so damaging are liable to remain with us as 1999 rolls along.

Here are some more danger signs.

FALTERING ECONOMY AND EARNINGS

As 1999 begins, both of the driving forces of the long bull market—the strong economy and impressive earnings growth—seem to be in trouble for the first time in years, continuing to be negatively affected by the international crises. By the third quarter of 1998, earnings growth had not only slowed, but actually *declined* an average of 3.3 percent, the worst showing since the recession of 1990.

WANING CONSUMER CONFIDENCE?

With consumers having so much of their net worth in the stock market, much of their record-high confidence in the 1990s stemmed from their belief they had discovered a sure-fire money machine. No wonder then that the stock market correction in 1998 had a considerable effect in dampening their confidence. New housing construction dropped significantly thereafter, as did retail sales. By October 1998, the Consumer Confidence Index had dropped from a record 132 earlier in the year to 117.

The market's rally back to its previous highs in the winter did improve consumer confidence again. However, economic numbers showed that consumer spending was exceeding consumer income for the first time in many years, an unsustainable situation.

In the meantime, as soon as corporations recognized their sales and earnings were being adversely affected by the international crisis, they began laying off employees and closing plants. If that trend becomes more noticeable, it will not be welcome news to consumers, and therefore not good news for the consumer-driven economy.

A BANKING CRISES IN 1999?

In 1799, John Adams said, "Banks have done more injury to the morality, prosperity, and wealth of the nation than they will ever do good."

Perhaps Adams's concerns in 1799 should be our concerns in 1999.

The banking industry has an appalling record of allowing excess greed to overwhelm its judgment, with the government periodically having to step in with taxpayer dollars to prevent a complete collapse of the financial system. Scares have included high-interest loans to struggling third-world countries in the 1970s, loans that had no hope of being paid back. Banks, trying to hide the situation, were finally ordered to write-off billions of dollars of the bad loans, and so-called Brady bonds had to be issued to cover the rest and bail the banks out. Bank greed involving junk bond financing and careless loans in the

1980s resulted in the infamous S&L scandals and ultimate collapse of the S&L industry, with the bailout costing taxpayers billions of dollars. Greed and reckless loans to developers, takeover artists, and other speculators, as the economy approached its peak prior to the 1990 recession, resulted in the failure and closing of 169 banks. Most of the rest had to be bailed out and restructured by the FDIC, in a very close call for the banking system.

The greed of banks may be setting the financial system up for similar problems as this decade draws to a close.

There used to be definite partitions, by law, between financial institutions. Banks made their profits by taking in deposits and loaning the money out at interest. Insurance companies took in premiums for life and casualty insurance policies, and invested the proceeds conservatively to make sure the money would be available to pay off on the policies. Brokerage firms sold stocks and bonds to raise money for corporations and governments. Mutual funds took in investors' money directly and invested it for them in a diversified portfolio of stocks or bonds.

With powerful lobbying by the banking industry, those safety barriers were gradually removed in the 1990s. Banks and insurance companies wanted to get in on the huge profits being produced by the biggest bull market ever. Once the barriers were down, a wild surge of merger and acquisition activity took place, with banks scrambling to buy up brokerage firms, mutual funds, and each other.

Up to their necks now in promoting investments to their customers, and operating trading departments for their own assets, caution and the conservative care usually associated with banks and insurance companies is difficult to find.

The banking industry received several scares in 1998: losses on international loans; losses on their own international trading; losses from financing hedge funds, which then also had losses in *their* international trading; warnings from participants that banks do not even understand the complex, high-risk, derivatives trading they are either directly or indirectly exposed to; and warnings from the Federal Reserve that banks had become too lax and needed to tighten their lending practices or face losses from problem loans if the economy slows.

Let's add one other potential catalyst for a 1999 bear market to the mix.

HERE COMES Y2K

The world is now entering a zone it has been anticipating with some fear, the time zone in which the infamous Y2K computer glitch comes into play. As everyone must realize by now, because of memory restrictions of earlier computers, software programs written prior to the last year or two record the year field in only two digits. At the end of 1999, those programs will read 00 as 1900 rather than the year 2000. It's widely feared the government and major corporations, from banks and brokerage firms to hospitals and airlines, have put off fixing the problem to the point that many won't get it all done in time. Horror stories abound over business grinding to a halt in important areas if even 90 percent of computer programs worldwide are rewritten in time, but 10 percent are not. Almost unnoticed is the cost that is associated with fixing the problem, costs that will come out of already declining corporate earnings. In November 1998, Citicorp, Sun Trust, and a dozen other large banks revealed in filings to the SEC that they would be spending $1.7 billion to fix their computer systems to recognize dates correctly and avert troubles in 2000.

Companies, scrambling to avert disaster, have now become more concerned about other people's Y2K problems that could make their own fixed systems inoperable anyway. In November 1998, giant British consumer goods manufacturer Unilever completed changes it believes will fix its computers, and set aside 1999 for testing and debugging. However, it then discovered that 25 percent of its 80,000 suppliers had not done anything to become Y2K compliant, and Unilever's Chairman

Niall FitzGerald said, "The time left for them to get their systems compliant is not enough." Dutch airline KLM said it plans to cancel all flights around December 31, 1999, since, although its systems are now compliant, it is certain that European air traffic control systems are unprepared. KLM's CIO Max Rens said, "We don't trust the governments. We think they are too late." Credit card giant Visa expects telephone systems in emerging countries in Asia and Latin America are likely to collapse.

No one seems to know if the problems will materialize or not, but it's certainly another uncertainty for an already high-risk market in 1999.

PUT IT ALL TOGETHER

As of late 1998, the U.S. stock market has gone for the longest period in its history without a serious bear market to correct the excesses, so, not surprisingly, in the process the excesses have reached never-before-seen extremes.

Put those extremes—record-high stock valuations, record overbought conditions, record public participation, record allocation of the nation's wealth to the stock market—into the same pot with currency and economic collapses around the world that have spread from Japan, Hong Kong and the rest of Asia to Russia, and on to Latin America. Stir in already slowing U.S. corporate earnings and growing layoffs. Spice it a bit with banking system and Y2K worries. Add a pinch of reality created by 1998's wake-up call in the market. Allow to simmer a while, and what do you get? A big chocolate cake with lots of frosting with which to continue the endless party to even higher records of overvaluation, as Wall Street would have us believe? Or an ugly mix that's likely to get thrown out to the bears?

It seems clear that it's not a question of "if" and that there's not too much room in which to place "when" leaving the main question "how much."

CHAPTER 13

LOOK OUT BELOW?

What should we expect from the next bear market?

The last two, in 1987 and 1990, were the quickest bear markets ever seen, all over in three months. If we have to have one, one of those would be nice.

Or would it? Looking back on them with the benefit of 20-20 hindsight, knowing the market recovered, and within a couple of years was back to its previous peak, gives investors confidence a bear market like those would be easy enough to hold through. Those of us who experienced them know better.

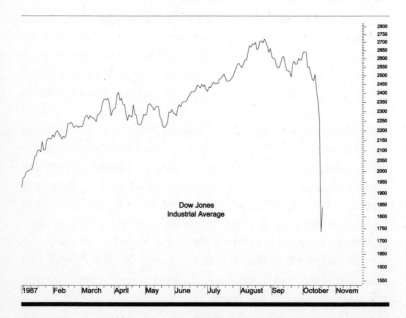

Dow Jones
Industrial Average

Just for fun, in the chart on the previous page, we've removed the knowledge that the market recovered so quickly and look at the 1987 bear market as it looked to participants at the time.

Now, factor in what investors were hearing at the time. Gone was all semblance of bullishness or confidence on Wall Street or in the media. The market's three-month decline of 17 percent leading up to the actual crash had pretty well dampened all bullishness. Keep in mind that investors then had not been treated to a record eight-year bull market and were well aware that serious bear markets come along every three years or so.

When the nervousness, created by the losses already experienced, was followed by the Black Monday one-day crash of an additional 24 percent, it was not an inspiring scene. To begin with, the one-day crash was worse than the one-day crash that had occurred within the granddaddy of all bear markets, the 1929 market crash. It also came after the market had reached its highest level of overvaluation since 1929. Not surprisingly, the combination was widely interpreted as a guarantee that something like the Great Depression would follow as surely as night follows day.

Adding to the despair, the market was wildly out of control during the actual crash. Only much later did investors learn how close the entire financial system had come to total meltdown that day. Sell orders so swamped the trading floor right from the open that the NYSE was unable to get all thirty Dow stocks open for trading until two hours into the session, by which time the Dow was already down 9 percent. Program traders continued to dump in wave after wave of sell programs throughout the day as successive "protective stops" were hit. Trading in many stocks was repeatedly halted because at times there were no buyers *at any price* for them. Floor specialists, who are supposed to step into the breach and take the other side of sell orders when there are no buyers, did not have the capital to do so under such a deluge. For instance, the specialist firm that was supposed to provide an orderly market in twenty-seven different stocks had capital of $12 million and access to credit of another $40 million. Yet volume in just two of the stocks in which the firm was supposed to make the market, USX and Shell Oil, totaled $250 million that day.

Such is the stuff of which panics are made. Telephone systems were totally inadequate for the volume of calls trying to get through. Investors could not reach their brokers, and those few who did, or went to their broker's office, could get no information since the brokers themselves could get no information. The plunges were triggering margin calls, and panicked floor brokers were simply selling margined investors' positions out, without trying to have the margin call made to the investor for more cash.

A friend of mine was a longtime broker at a Merrill Lynch office at the time. He told me later that as the plunge worsened that day, he and most of his fellow brokers simply abandoned their desks and went out for lunch breaks that lasted through the rest of the trading day. Their nerves could not handle the decimation taking place in their own and their customers' accounts. They dreaded the occasional calls that were getting through since they had no answers for their customers. They had been trained primarily to sell "products" and to placate customers' worries with encouraging words, but there was no way to smooth over what was happening. They left it to their secretaries to tell customers they were "in a strategy meeting and unavailable."

President Reagan, cabinet members, the heads of major corporations, and the president of the NYSE, were out in force trying to calm the panic that evening. The atmosphere in the country was pure fear—and for good reason as it turned out, when it was revealed months later that those in charge were as panicked as the country they were trying to calm, not knowing what it all meant or how it could be resolved.

The following day brought little relief. Encouraged by the previous evening's statements from Wall Street, the White House, and the Federal Reserve that all was well, and deliberate buying by some corporations to create a bounce, bargain hunters did come in on the buy side, and by 10:30 a.m. the Dow was up 11 percent. However, selling immediately took over again, and buyers disappeared. Unable, *or unwilling*, to take the other side of so many sell orders, many specialists simply halted trading in the stocks for which they were responsible. Sears stopped trading at 11:12 a.m., Kodak at 11:28, Phillip Morris and IBM at 11:30, Dow Chemical at 11:43, and so on.

Understand what that means. With the stock halted, an investor *cannot* sell. The rest of the market may be falling, but the owner of a halted stock can only watch helplessly, knowing only that when his or her stock begins trading again it's going to be at a much lower price. For the rest of investors, with important Dow and S&P 500 stocks halted, there was no accurate way of knowing just how badly the market was doing. More panic.

The market did begin to rally over coming days, but the most widely held view was that the plunge would soon resume, with support all the way down at 1000 on the Dow, another 45 percent lower. That was the level at which the Dow had struggled for so many years before breaking up through it, and the expectation was that 1000 would now be firm support. Even from that level it was expected the market would do no better than trade sideways since in the economy the dominant talk was of a second Great Depression that would last for years.

Investors that were still holding at the time of the final crash certainly held through *it*, not by choice, but because there was virtually no way to get out. But current investors who believe they would have still been willing to hold *after* the crash—with portfolios decimated, even the conservative Dow already down 36 percent, and the dominant talk being of another severe leg down and the onset of a second Great Depression—are kidding themselves.

Investors were able to get out *after* the plunge, and did so in droves. Keep in mind that though the conservative stocks of the Dow lost 36.1 percent in the 1987 bear market, it's estimated that the average stock lost closer to 60 percent. Charts we've already shown reveal the degree to which money flowed out of mutual funds for several years after the crash. Investors' nerves and confidence were simply shattered by the experience.

So, don't let 20-20 hindsight that revealed much later that the Black Monday crash was actually the bear market low, lead you to believe that you would have expected that to be the case at the time, or that you would have been one of the rare individuals who continued to hold until the market recovered to its previous highs two years later.

A BEAR MARKET IS A BEAR

Usually, either they are brief but ugly, and panic investors out at the bottom, or they grind their way down for several years, wearing down investors' tolerance for pain until they give up in disgust at the low. Panicked out or disgusted out still adds up to buying high and selling low.

The only way to avoid being mauled by a bear is to avoid the animal in the first place. To deliberately decide to contend with it, confident the mauling will be endurable, or brief, or that this particular animal will be toothless, is foolhardy. Besides, why endure

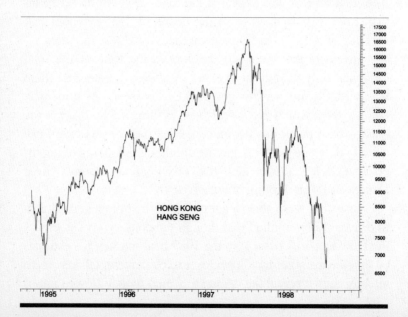

HONG KONG
HANG SENG

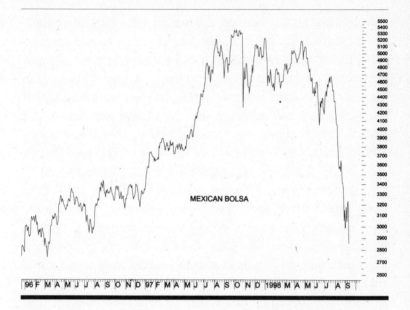

MEXICAN BOLSA

it, when all it takes is a phone call or two to escape its clutches? Afraid to miss more gains if the bear is slow to arrive?

Let's use a little hindsight ourselves.

Did it matter to investors in Hong Kong, or Mexico, or Japan, or Thailand, or Korea, or Russia, or Brazil, or Argentina in 1998 that they had stayed in for the final gains in 1997?

Did it matter to U.S. investors who bailed out at the 1974, 1978, 1982, 1987, 1990 bear market lows that they got the last six months, the last year, or even the last two years of bull market gains? They didn't keep them.

THAT'S NOT YOGI AROUND THE BEND

Analysts who compare current conditions to those of 1929 can expect gibes and sarcasm. Wall Street just won't stand for such comparisons, and understandably so. It can handle occasional investor fear of bear markets like those seen in 1987 and 1990. It's easy enough to point out, with the wonderful advantage of 20-20 hindsight, that they were over in three months, and *if*

investors had simply held on, the market came back in a couple
of years. It's more difficult, but they can even handle comparisons to normal bear markets that lasted several years and saw
declines of 45 percent or more on the Dow, *and 65 percent in
the average investor's portfolio.* Again with the advantage of
hindsight, they can point out that even those experiences did
end and the market came back. Of course, they conveniently
ignore the fact that while *any* of the bear market experiences
were being endured, such an outcome was far from assured.

However, when it comes to downplaying the 1929–1932
stock market crash, they have no wriggle room. There simply
were *no* survivors, so even to say that the market was back to
its 1929 peak twenty-six years later, in 1955, is meaningless.
Thus their only defense is to resort to ridicule and sarcasm that
anyone could consider such an event happening again.

Investors certainly don't want to hear such comparisons.
It's human nature when we're enjoying a good time to resent
any attempt to warn us of subsequent repercussions that will
result from the excess partying.

However, we *have* to look at the shadow being cast by
what is lurking around the corner this time. If ever there were a
bear to be avoided, it looks as if the next one will be it.

We've shown you the comparisons of current conditions to
those at previous major market tops. Let's look at them again
for a moment, not just as evidence that the market is more dan-
gerously at risk of a bear market than it has ever been before,
but to see how conditions so closely resemble those of 1929,
suggesting the next bear market is likely to be the most severe
bear market since that monster.

GOLDILOCKS

We spoke earlier of how similar the "fairy tale" in the 1920s
was to the current story, providing the basis in each period for
investors to believe "this time is different, valuations don't matter, and the bull market can simply last forever." In the 1990s,

it's been the introduction of computers and automation, which will supposedly allow companies to produce increasingly more goods with ever-fewer employees, allowing earnings to grow forever, while the endless stream of exciting new consumer products, from computers to entertainment, will create endless sales growth. In the 1920s, it was the introduction of electricity into homes and factories that would provide the same production benefits and the new products.

In the 1920s, the enthusiasm for stocks drove the market ever higher for a then record period of eight years without an intervening bear market. In the 1990s, a similarly euphoric market has been driven ever higher and, in 1998, achieved, and then exceeded, the 1920s record run of eight years without a bear market. Wall Street even trotted out an actual fairy tale to describe 1998 conditions, referring to the economy as a "Goldilocks economy," neither too hot nor too cold, but just right for many more years of good times.

In the 1920s, the long stretch without an intervening bear market to correct the excesses allowed those excesses to build to

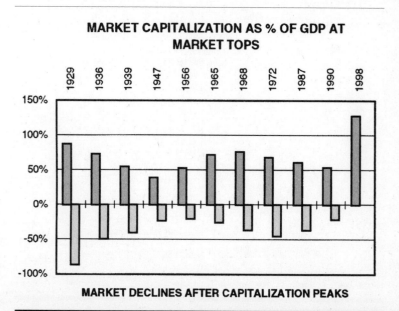

levels never seen before or since. *Until now* that is, when virtually all 1929 excesses have been equaled or surpassed. Perhaps Wall Street storytellers should have recalled that not only did the 1929 market run immediately into the most vicious bear ever, but that even Goldilocks eventually ran into the three bears.

Probably the most revealing similarity to 1929 is the degree to which the stock market now dominates the economy, as shown on the chart on the previous page, with market capitalization equal to 128 percent of Gross Domestic Product, compared to the then ominous 87 percent at the 1929 market top.

We also want to revisit the following chart, which shows how the eight-year bull market of the 1990s has spiked the market up to a degree only seen once before—in 1929!

From its market peak in 1929, the DJIA lost 86 percent of its value to its bear market low in 1932. Such a decline from the 1999 peak sounds impossible—and probably is. Let's hope so.

However, we have to be realistic. Not even counting that 86 percent plunge, since 1900 there have been seven bear markets

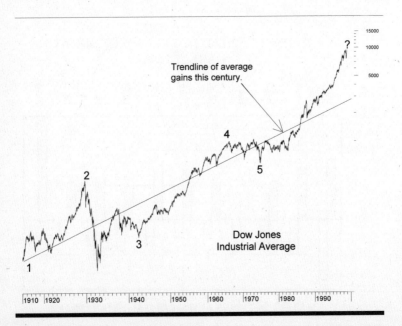

Trendline of average gains this century.

Dow Jones
Industrial Average

in which the Dow lost an average of 45 percent. At none of them was the market close to being as overvalued and overextended as it was in 1929, *and as it is in 1999*. On that basis alone, a bear market decline from current levels of *between* 45 and 90 percent has to be recognized as a real possibility.

Another way to gauge the risk is to realize that historically the S&P 500 has traded as high as 2.5 times its book value, 22.7 times its earnings, and 38.7 times its dividend at previous market tops, and as low as 1 times its book value, 7 times its earnings, and 11 times its dividend yield at bear market lows. Its historical *average* valuation level has been 1.6 times its book value, 14 times its earnings, and 24 times its dividend yield.

With the S&P 500 now trading at never-before-seen valuation levels of 5.9 times its book value, 31 times its earnings, and 69 times its dividend yield, *it would take a 72 percent decline to get the S&P 500 just back to selling at its average price/book value ratio. It would take a 50 percent decline to get it back to just its average valuation level based on its earnings, and a 65 percent decline to get it back to its average valuation level based on its price/dividend yield.*

As large as those declines are, the fact remains that the least that should be expected of a bear market would be for it to carry overvaluations down to average valuations, which represent neither boom times nor bust.

We have to depend on the Federal Reserve to prevent something worse from happening, like a repeat of 1929. The Fed's mandate is to maintain stability in the nation's banking system and economy through control of interest rates and the money supply. Its mandate is definitely *not* to maintain stability in the stock market. Federal Reserve Chairman Greenspan has frequently warned of "irrational exuberance" in the market in recent years, and reminded investors that *they* will bear any losses that result from their decisions to ignore the risk.

However, a loss of wealth in the next bear market similar to that seen in the 1929–1932 bear would surely cause a repeat of the Great Depression in the economy. And the Fed's mandate *is* to protect the economy. So, although the Fed totally failed to prevent the calamity in 1929, we believe the Fed has learned and now has the knowledge and ability to prevent a recurrence of the Great Depression. And to that extent anyway, in a severe stock market collapse back toward average valuations, the market should benefit from the Fed's efforts to protect the economy.

There are skeptics, of course, who believe the Fed's easy-money policies that supported the long and strong economic boom of the 1990s bear ominous similarities to its easy-money policies of the 1920s. Their scenario is that the economy of the United States, as well as its stock market, is a bubble of excessive debt that will pop just as it did in 1929.

In any event, conditions point to the next bear market being imminent and likely to be of the most severe variety.

CHAPTER 14

PUBLIC INVESTORS VERSUS WALL STREET

Public investors will not be able to prepare for and handle both bull and bear markets until they realize that all is not as it's made to seem in the securities industry. It's an ugly truth, but Wall Street professionals and insiders do not compete so much with each other for profits as they strive to take their profits from public investors. I wish there were some way to avoid this unpleasantness, but there is no way investors will succeed to the degree we believe they can without knowing the tilt of the playing field.

The truths are deep rooted, and we will need a brief but interesting trip back in time to bring today's picture into sharper focus.

THE PROPHETIC FIRST OFFERING IN THE UNITED STATES

It took place in 1790. The new nation's economy was in shambles. The value of its currency, the dollar, had collapsed under the weight of financing the Revolutionary War and was being honored at one-tenth of its face value. To solve the problem, Alexander Hamilton proposed to Congress that it issue bonds and use the proceeds to redeem dollars at face value. He correctly believed that would restore the dollar's value and the creditworthiness of the new nation.

History tells us that, "a speculative frenzy broke out among those on the inside, particularly members of Congress, which immediately adjourned." Congressmen, and others who knew of Hamilton's proposal, hired boats and worked their way up and down the Atlantic Coast buying up undervalued dollars for ten cents each from the unsuspecting public. Only when they were loaded up with them did they return and begin their congressional debate, which approved the government's first sale of bonds, the proceeds of which were used to redeem those dollars at face value.

With that very first public offering in the United States, the insiders positioned their own portfolios first, and made huge profits at the expense of an uninformed public.

It was just the beginning!

LET'S START THE BIDDING ON MOLASSES, TOBACCO—AND STOCKS?

In the late 1700s, Wall Street was the center of commercial activity in the fledgling city of New York. The street had been named in the 1600s in deference to a mud wall erected to ward off Indians. Its location, running from the docks on the East River, attracted a hodgepodge of merchants who brokered molasses, furs, tobacco, cotton, and other commodities. They made a profit by running auctions to bring buyers and sellers together, taking a commission from both sides on each trade. Between the auctions, they brokered smaller lots "over the counter" at their individual businesses.

As is true today, prices changed up and down not only based on the present value of the commodities, but even more so on expectations of future supplies. When ships loaded with molasses were lost at sea, molasses prices jumped in anticipation there would be shortages. Favorable weather in the tobacco-growing areas caused the price of tobacco to fall in anticipation of a surplus of tobacco flooding the market.

It was fairly common for the merchant-auctioneers, and others, to start rumors moving through the crowd of storms at sea, or problems on the cotton plantations, in an attempt to move prices up or down in accordance with their own agenda. You're no doubt familiar with similar tactics in today's markets. Traders love to get rumors started that George Soros is buying or selling bonds or Deutchmarks, or XYZ company is a takeover target, or central banks are selling gold, or whatever will move the market to support their positions.

When the government began selling bonds, and financiers began raising capital to found banks and other businesses by selling shares to the public, the tobacco and fur-trading merchant-brokers on Wall Street put in an inventory of stocks and bonds, and began buying and selling them over the counter. Over the next few years, as more and more entrepreneurs and financiers turned to the public to raise capital, increasing the number of stocks and bonds available, some merchant-brokers dropped their other activities to concentrate solely on the brokering of securities.

As they had previously done with cotton, tobacco, and furs, those brokers soon banded together to hold regularly scheduled auctions just for securities. In the beginning, the auctions took place outdoors, at noontime, under a buttonwood tree in front of 68 Wall Street. The public, being retail customers, were not allowed to attend the auctions. They had to arrange for a broker to handle the transaction for them on a commission basis.

As time went by, it evolved that certain brokers tended to specialize in certain stocks, and other brokers learned they'd usually find the largest inventory and best prices if they sought out the specialist in the stock they wanted to trade. To make himself easier to locate, each specialist began to station himself at a particular spot, usually a specific lamppost. From his specialist's post he carried on the auctions for the stocks he handled.

That was the beginning of the modern-day securities industry on Wall Street. Believe it or not, not an awful lot has changed in the 200 years since.

MANIPULATORS AND SWINDLERS—OLD STYLE

The shenanigans of market manipulators of past eras has been well-chronicled elsewhere, so we won't dwell on them. However, a brief reminder and overview of their tactics for today's new investors is important if we are to be street smart.

The big names of earlier eras included Andrew Carnegie, Judge William H. Moore, Jay Gould, Cornelius Vanderbilt, Jim Fisk, Daniel Drew, J. P. Morgan, John D. Rockefeller, James R. Keane, Joseph P. Kennedy, Bernard Baruch, Walter Chrysler, and hundreds more. They had great sport with the markets and the public.

THE CATTLE BROKER

Daniel Drew was a wealthy cattle broker who made his fortune brokering undernourished animals at extravagant prices for their owners. His method was to leave the cattle unfed and starving for several days prior to showing them to a prospective buyer. Then the night before, he'd give them all the salt they'd eat, and keep them away from water for the rest of the night. The next morning, just before the arrival of the buyer, he'd provide the starving and parched animals with all the water they could hold. The additional 100 pounds of water per head provided the seller, and Daniel the broker, with a substantial profit.

Daniel then turned his interest to the stock market. He used his wealth to bail out the New York & Erie Railroad after a stock market crash had it on the ropes. Becoming the president of the railroad, he almost immediately began manipulating its stock for his own profits, an occupation he pursued for many years. His methods were quite simple, but clever.

For example, during a period of good times for railroads, when Drew wanted to own all the New York & Erie stock he could accumulate, he instead sold all the Erie stock he owned, and sold short all he could borrow for the purpose. He then spread rumors and "inside information" that the company was running into severe problems. The stock began to drop, eventually declining from 95 all the way to 47. At that point, Drew covered his short positions, doubling his money. He then bought heavily at the depressed price, acquiring the portfolio of stock he originally wanted, but at half price. He subsequently released inside information that the company had solved its problems, and only golden years lay ahead. That maneuver also had *its* intended effect, and the stock subsequently traded as high as $200.

For the next twenty-five years, Drew, frequently with the connivance of Vanderbilt and Jim Fisk, repeatedly orchestrated investors' interest in the stock so they'd buy heavily at high prices, as high as $200, and sell out at low prices, as low as $50, providing the supply and demand he and his cohorts needed so they could do just the opposite.

It's interesting that, in his later years, Drew was forced out of the Erie Railroad when he was caught raiding its treasury for his own use. Operating in the stock market as an outsider, his fortunes took a steep slide all the way into bankruptcy. The former cattle broker said at the time, "To speculate in Wall Street when you are no longer an insider is like buying cows in candlelight." He died broke and bitter.

THE STEEL MAN

John W. Gates, president of American Steel & Wire, and a group of associates quietly sold short a large amount of *his* company's stock. Gates then announced publicly that some of the company's mills would have to be closed down for a time due to a lack of orders. Privately, to a small group of friends at a party, he revealed that, "Business couldn't be better, but a group of us are short the stock." With the announcement of the plant closings, the stock began declining from the 60s into the 30s, where Gates and his associates covered their short positions, almost doubling their money, and then moved to the buy side to buy their stock back. Shortly thereafter, Gates reopened the mills, and the stock rose back to its old highs.

Such manipulations were not illegal at the time since until 1933, virtually no rules or regulations were in place. However, such flagrant abuse of investors has been illegal since 1933.

Therefore, in the modern-day market, when we see what seems to be similar attempts by corporate insiders to entice public investors in or out of their company's stock, it's comforting to know their buying or selling must be inspired by some motive other than their own profits.

PUBLICITY

The most important key to successful market manipulation in the early part of the century was the creation of misleading publicity. The classic reference book of market history, *The Stock Market,* in describing publicity as the major tool of manipulation of the old market, put it this way: "The purpose of publicity was primarily to attract the general public into the stock and keep it there until the manipulators had unloaded their holdings." News releases regarding earnings expectations, order backlogs, new product developments, and so forth were timed to coincide with whether the manipulators wanted the public to be buying or selling at the time. More sinister rumors and outright lies were frequently disseminated: "Tips and rumors, planted in receptive ears, found wide circulation, flying from trader to trader, eventually finding their way over the ticker service and into financial news columns. Why were they so often believed? Part of the answer, no doubt, was in the large extent of gullibility of the market in the 1920s."

HOW A BOOKIE BECAME AN ADVISOR TO KINGS

Bernard Baruch, who later became a wealthy philanthropist and advisor to kings and presidents, began his career as a runner for brokerage firm A. A. Houseman & Co. while also operating as a bookie for the famed stock manipulator James R. Keane. When J. P. Morgan, of the investment banking firm Drexel, Morgan & Co., organized the subsequently revealed "watering" of U.S. Steel shares, Keene was put in charge of promoting the watered stock to the public. He allowed his bookie, Baruch, to participate in a small way, and Baruch was hooked by the easy profits.

In his memoirs, *Baruch, My Own Story*, Baruch described as his first "big deal" on his own, the manipulation of Continental Tobacco shares. Tobacco baron James Duke, of American Tobacco fame, had set up a company, Continental Tobacco, which he intended to use in his ongoing battle to acquire Liggett & Myers and other tobacco companies. Thomas Ryan headed a syndicate that was also maneuvering to acquire tobacco companies. Ryan provided Baruch with $200,000 to use in manipulating the stock of Continental Tobacco. Baruch "enlisted the assistance" of two stockbrokers to handle his trades and assist with spreading rumors. For six weeks, he kept Continental shares alternately rallying and plunging, creating the kind of volatility that causes investors to give up in disgust. At the end of the six weeks, Baruch had the price of Continental shares down 33 percent. He wrote, "I also adopted the tactic of buying each time the stock was weak, and reselling it each time it rallied. This enabled me to make a net profit for myself even while pushing the price of Continental down 33 percent for the Ryan syndicate."

Ryan then told Baruch to stop the manipulative operation. He had shaken the Duke forces enough that they had reached an agreement with the Ryan syndicate on how they would split up the various tobacco company takeovers that were expected. It doesn't take much imagination to realize what was happening to public investors in tobacco stocks in the meantime, being manipulated to buy or sell to meet Baruch's agenda, with no idea of what was really going on.

Baruch's success in the Continental stock manipulation earned him a reputation and more "jobs," and he was soon a multimillionaire, friend, and advisor to kings and presidents.

Baruch could boast of such deliberate manipulation because manipulating the market through misleading publicity, like insider trading, was not illegal at the time.

THE FATHER OF A PRESIDENT

Joseph P. Kennedy made a famous fortune investing in and manipulating the market in the early part of the century. The story of his various manipulations, from the Yellow Cab Company to RKO Studios, has been well documented. Kennedy made a second fortune by selling short in the 1929–1932 bear market. His profits from the crash are estimated at up to $15 million, a staggering sum for the time. Other big winners included William Danforth, rumored to have made $7 million over just four days, and Ben Smith, said to have made $10 million in a month. Were they satisfied to simply make the massive profits available on the short side of such a market plunge? Not when the profit could be maximized with a little market manipulation.

Senator Burton Wheeler, of Montana, met Kennedy one day at the Harvard Club. He pointed out to Kennedy that Anaconda Copper had fallen all the way to $20 a share. Knowledgeable about Anaconda's large mining operations in his home state, Wheeler said he thought the stock was a bargain at that level. Kennedy told him not to buy the stock at *any* price. "It will be at $5 before we get through with it." He told Wheeler that a pool, of which he was a member, was manipulating the stock to cause everyone to bail out of it. Sure enough, the plunge in the already devastated shares of Anaconda continued until Kennedy's target was reached.

The manipulations were not for just a few "points," nor did they result in minor damage.

For instance, William Rockefeller, W. W. Rogers, E. H. Harriman, and Tom Lawson paid a total of $39 million for the copper properties that made up Amalgamated Copper. They then valued the combined companies for the public at $75 million, selling the shares at $100 each. Shortly thereafter, the bear market of 1901–1903 took place. Amalgamated Copper fell as low as 34. Lawson later admitted the stock that had been distributed to the public at up to three times that price was then reaccumulated by the original distributors.

It was not just individual stocks that were manipulated for huge profits, but the entire market. Of the bear market that began in 1906, brokerage firm partner Richard D. Wyckoff had this to say in his 1930 memoirs:

Late in 1905, a conference was held at the mansion of John D. Rockefeller at Lakewood, N.J. Measures were decided upon with the aim of inducing the public to buy in a volume that would create a market in which these large operators could successfully unload [to take their profits from the previous few years of bull market]. Union Pacific was already selling at 150. The plan was to make it available on a 10 percent margin basis. At the same time they would make Southern Pacific a 5 percent margin stock. This, it was expected, would create excitement and have the desired effect of raising the whole market. A few days after the meeting, floor brokers were amazed to see the two announcements. With the extra buying debt allowed, the public flooded their brokers with buy orders. Union Pacific jumped to the 190s in just a few days, and Southern Pacific from the low 60s into the 90s almost as quickly. The excitement spread through the market as anticipated, with everything going up. The action created by that manipulation produced the climactic top of the 1906 bull market. The average price of the twenty railroads reached 168, a figure that would not be seen again for many years. Into this strength, in which Harriman made $15,000,000 on his Union Pacific alone, the big operators, leading financiers, and banking institutions who understood what was happening, were able to clean house. Large estates that had tremendous holdings in the railroads were splitting the certificates up into smaller lots and liquidating them into the public demand.

No sooner had the Wall Street operators and investment banks unloaded their high-priced holdings into the public excitement they had artificially created, than the 1906–1907 bear market began, which produced a decline of 48.5 percent over the following two years.

Wyckoff not only pointed out how easily and often the public was duped into buying near the tops, in fact created the

tops with their excited buying, but also how they were tricked
into buying the dips on the way down, providing the volume for
those who were still selling, while not selling themselves until
the bear market had bottomed. Wyckoff described the bear market of 1902 and 1903:

> As it [U.S. Steel] went down, brokers advised
> their customers to buy more of this great investment,
> using their current shares as margin collateral to aver-
> age down. Thus many found themselves long 200
> shares, on margin, for every 100 originally held. And
> still the price declined as the bankers and big opera-
> tors unloaded their portfolios into the public buying.
> As their customers' margin collateral declined, the
> brokers merely sold them out.

Of the eventual bear market bottom Wyckoff said:

> With U.S. Steel at $10 [down from its previous
> high of 50], my partner and I took pads and pencils
> and began to do some figuring. We calculated that the
> decline in the market had done its job of wiping out
> the previous overvaluation. We went into action right
> away. We bought some Steel as low as 8 5/8, within a
> quarter point of the lowest it had ever traded. Not long
> thereafter, Steel and the rest of the market began to
> creep up. Vast accumulation was again underway.
> Rockefeller ordered a private telegraph wire run into
> his house, the old man was socking away bundles of
> Steel certificates in one of the downtown vaults. The
> Morgans were now on the buy side, buying heavily
> and quietly telling their friends to get aboard again.

> We tried to interest some of our public clients.
> They would have none of it. The general market was,
> as usual, being manipulated now to keep the public
> fearful and out of it, until the bankers' portfolios could
> be loaded up again at the low prices. So when the

market advanced too much, as the bankers bought and some of the public ventured in, the advance was promptly knocked on the head by manipulative selling. The result was a narrow whipsawing market in which traders, long or short, could not make any money, but the accumulators could continue to accumulate. These conditions make the public very bearish. It's a well known principle of manipulation that more people can be tired out and made disgusted with their holdings, and thus induced to sell at the low prices, in a stagnant market, than are shaken out or scared out by the prior decline. In a decline many will hold on hoping for a rally that will let them out at higher prices. If they get a rally they don't sell out because the rally makes them bullish again. But, the whipsawing at the bottom grinds them down and they do give up.

And so the next bull phase got underway without the public participating until Steel was trading above 40 again.

INSISTING ON BUYING HIGH

E. H. Harriman was asked if he could unload a substantial amount of a stock for its wealthy owner at an average price of 70 if the owner first spread rumors about the stock and did some buying to manipulate the price up to 80. Harriman said no, he could not. However, he said, "I could readily manipulate it up to 120 and then unload it back to 80 for an average price of 100." His reasoning was that a ten point rise would not attract much attention, but a fifty-point rise would attract enormous attention and have the public clamoring for the stock. Any amount of stock could then be sold, "as people who thought themselves shrewd would keeping buying the dips as it fell to 80, thinking it looked cheap compared to where it had been at 120."

THE EXTENT OF THE CHICANERY

Don't fall for the securities industry's attempt to whitewash the facts and rewrite history. They would have you believe that stock and market manipulation was rare, and involved only a few "bad apples" and a few stocks.

However. according to 1933 congressional investigations undertaken after the 1929 stock market crash, in 1929 alone, *just one year*, 107 of the most prominent stocks on the New York Stock Exchange were manipulated one or more times, *just by pools that included members of the NYSE itself.* The manipulated stocks included those of some of the largest, most popular companies of the time: American Tobacco, Canada Dry, Chrysler, Colgate, Curtiss Wright, Fox Theaters, B.F. Goodrich, Montgomery Ward, National Cash Register, National Steel, North American Aviation, Packard, RCA, Remington Rand, Sinclair Oil, Standard Brands, Standard Oil of California, Studebaker, Union Carbide, and on and on.

Congress admitted it had uncovered just the tip of the iceberg. Their figures included only manipulations that congressional investigators were able to uncover, only "pool" manipulations in which members of the NYSE were involved, and only the one year of 1929. There are no accurate figures of how many manipulations by NYSE members were not uncovered; how many stocks were manipulated by pools that included members of other exchanges, nonmember firms and banks, corporate insiders, or the private operators like Joseph P. Kennedy and Bernard Baruch; or how many took place in other years. It's safe to assume that the numbers were huge and that the majority of public investors were seriously affected.

Professing their shock at what they had learned, Congress passed legislation in 1933 and again in 1934 to bring about regulation of the securities industry.

CHAPTER 15

ABOUT THOSE REGULATIONS

REGULATIONS AT LAST

For 140 years, the securities industry had been virtually unwatched and unregulated. However, complaints after the 1929–1932 market crash—that bear raiding, bulling of stocks, fictitious trading, pools, unfair use of inside information, misleading publicity, and myriad other manipulations had massively defrauded the public—forced Congress to investigate. Professing to be stunned by what they learned (even though Representatives and Senators had often been members of the manipulative pools and syndicates), Congress passed the 1933 Truth in Securities Act, which basically required that publicly traded companies provide more and better information about their operations, financial condition, and insider trading, and do so in a timely manner. In 1934, Congress passed the Securities Exchange Act, aimed at ending fraudulent trading of securities, by regulating the stock exchanges and brokerage firms themselves.

Unless the abuse was planned and systemic, you'd think an industry would welcome legislation aimed at ending the fraudulent abuse of its customers. However, Sam Rayburn, speaker of the house at the time, said that Richard Whitney, the president of the New York Stock Exchange mounted, "the most powerful lobbying effort ever organized against a bill," in an effort to prevent its passage.

As a result of Wall Street's lobbying efforts, the legislation was watered down significantly, but the abuses were even more than Congress could abide, and federal regulation of the securities industry did finally arrive. The Securities and Exchange Commission, the SEC, was created to interpret and enforce the regulations.

Can you imagine the public's shock when President Roosevelt announced the name of the person he was appointing as the first chairman of the SEC, with its mandate to clean up the securities industry, and end the prior 140 years of financial abuse of investors?

Joseph P. Kennedy.

During the previous elections, Kennedy had taken time away from his Wall Street shenanigans to campaign heavily for Roosevelt on the hope of being named secretary of the treasury. He was disappointed and bitter when he didn't get that appointment. But over widespread howls of indignation, this Wall Street operator, who had told associates, "We better get all we can before Congress wakes up and passes laws against this stuff," was named as the man responsible for overseeing the industry.

The appointment brought shock waves in the media. Wall Street columnist John T. Flynn wrote, "I say it isn't true. It is impossible. It could not happen."

But it did.

FINALLY, PROTECTION?

Kennedy's actions amazed many. He called in the nervous heads of Wall Street brokerage firms and investments banks, as well as corporate executives and insiders, many of whom would be guilty of fraud under the new regulations. To their great surprise, he informed them the SEC would not undertake investigations of their past operations. That decision was providential for Kennedy as well since his own misdeeds would also fade into the mists of time.

To Wall Street's further surprise, Kennedy also told them he was not interested in having the SEC police the securities industry, but in having the industry police itself. The SEC would develop guidelines, and further, would do so based on input and suggestions from the industry, but the industry would be self-regulated.

Understandably, Wall Street breathed a huge sigh of relief.

WHITEWASHING

The securities industry spent the period after the introduction of regulations clothing its activities in a badly needed appearance of respectability. The exchanges announced reforms aimed at leveling the playing field for investors. In 1939, the National Association of Securities Dealers (NASD) was organized and given responsibility for testing, registering, and policing individual stockbrokers. As the name implies, the NASD was, and is, an organization of brokerage firms controlled by its members. Congress also designated the NASD as the SRO, or Self-Regulating Organization, for over-the-counter stocks (stocks that do not trade on the exchanges).

The whitewashing wasn't totally smooth going, however. Some prominent members were unwilling to lay low or cover up their activities for even a brief period.

Richard Whitney, president of the New York Stock Exchange during the period when Congress was debating regulations, was one of Wall Street's most respected leaders. His brokerage firm, Richard Whitney & Co., was a prominent firm on the Street.

Yet in the morning of March 8, 1938, four years after regulations and the SEC came into being, trading on the NYSE was halted for an announcement: "Brokerage firm Richard Whitney & Co. is suspended for conduct inconsistent with just and equitable trade."

Lawsuits by customers had revealed that Whitney and his firm were still involved in widespread activities to defraud investors. Their losses far exceeded the firm's ability to make good. Whitney and the firm were expelled from the NYSE, were forced by lawsuits into bankruptcy, and Whitney served time in prison.

The episode did little to calm investors' suspicions of Wall Street and the greed of those who controlled it. If Whitney of all people, prominent and respected, a recent president of the NYSE itself, was still carrying on as before, what could be expected of the rest of the industry, and just how much could be expected from the new regulations?

But enough of the past. Let's look at how well regulations control the industry in current times.

CHAPTER 16

TODAY'S WALL STREET

Do we even recognize the many faces of brokerage firms in the modern market?

- Brokerage firms are the members of the various stock exchanges and dominate their boards of governors, thus determining how the exchanges will operate.
- Brokerage firms are the "specialists" on the exchange trading floors, who make the markets in the specific stocks they've been assigned.
- Brokerage firms are the members of the National Association of Securities Dealers (NASD), which is the designated watchdog of the over-the-counter stock market, *and* the owner of the NASDAQ, which is the stock exchange for over-the-counter stocks.
- Brokerage firms are underwriters of new issues of stock, and are thus important as raisers of capital for corporations.
- Brokerage firms are traders in the markets for their own accounts, and indeed the majority of many firm's profits come from such trading.
- Brokerage firms are owners and managers of proprietary mutual funds that they sell to their customers.
- Brokerage firms are "inventors" and promoters of new financial products that are sold to their customers, products such as limited partnerships, CMOs (commercialized mortgage obligations), tax shelters,

STRIPS, LYONS (Liquid Yield Option Notes), and wrap accounts.

- Brokerage firms are middlemen, or wholesalers of stock to institutions like mutual funds, pension plans, banks, and other brokerage firms.
- Brokerage firms act like banks, by holding customer cash deposits and making margin loans to investors.
- And, oh yes, brokerage firms are brokers for retail customers, recommending stocks and arranging for the public's transactions to take place.

The conflicts of interest, opportunities, and temptations to deliberately take advantage of the overlapping responsibilities would tempt an angel.

For example, critics claim brokerage firms use their research recommendations and retail broker operations to artificially create public demand and support for companies that are customers of their investment banking divisions.

Other critics are concerned that brokerage firms are allowed to trade for their own accounts, operate as dealers of stocks, and also as brokers for the transactions of retail customers, claiming it is impossible to carry out such conflicting duties without abuses taking place.

Therefore, regulators insist on separation of brokerage firm operations.

How poorly those separations work is demonstrated only too often.

TRADING AGAINST THEIR CUSTOMERS

Just recently, in 1996, after a two-year investigation of the NASDAQ stock exchange and its owner *and* regulator, the NASD, the Justice Department and the SEC released reports that were scathing indictments of both. The reports confirmed years of complaints that NASDAQ market makers had routinely traded in front of their customers orders, failed to honor investors' orders at quoted prices, delayed reporting trades to trick customers about true prices, and threatened each other with retaliation to prevent anyone from straying from the game. Regarding the NASD, the organization responsible for policing the NASDAQ, the report said, "the NASD was aware of the facts and circumstances. . . . The NASD's response was to engage in public denials . . . to discredit complaints it should have recognized to be well-founded . . . by its inaction failed to satisfy its responsibilities as a Self Regulating Organization."

The report hardly surprised critics.

The Justice Department warned it had sufficient evidence to bring charges against thirty-seven brokerage firms that operate as market makers in NASDAQ stocks, for defrauding their customers of billions. The SEC suggested that the firms engage in settlement discussions. In November 1998, a settlement was announced wherein the thirty-seven firms, including some of the biggest names on Wall Street—Merrill Lynch, Goldman Sachs, Charles Schwab & Co., Salomon Smith Barney, and so on—provided a $1.03 billion restitution fund for defrauded investors.

A PIECE OF THE ROCK FALLS ON INVESTORS

Just two years prior, in 1995, the Justice Department brought criminal fraud charges against Prudential Securities, the country's fifth largest brokerage firm. The charges were that Prudential had knowingly defrauded customers to whom it had sold $8 billion worth of limited partnerships, those popular vehicles that allow small investors to take part in large real estate and leasing ventures. The evidence was clear and overwhelming as the case got underway, and Prudential quickly settled out of court, admitting the criminal wrongdoing, and setting up a $1.2 billion restitution fund.

As the Justice Department and the SEC broadened their investigations, Paine Webber agreed to pay $292 million in restitution to settle similar charges related to the sale of $3 billion of its limited partnerships. Soon thereafter, Merrill Lynch, Dean Witter Reynolds, and Lehman Brothers negotiated out-of-court settlements on comparable charges related to the sale of their limited partnerships.

LIMITED PARTNERSHIPS

I don't want to get started on limited partnerships (LPs) because they are a pet peeve of mine with the brokerage industry. But they are one of the biggest causes of damage to investors, and have been proved to often be promoted by misleading if not fraudulent methods. Readers need to be aware of the hazard.

It's estimated that the public poured more than $138 billion (yes, $138,000,000,000) into LPs over the years, with 30 percent of the total coming from their individual retirement accounts. In fact, when the IRS approved the introduction of individual retirement accounts (IRAs), which allowed $2000 tax-deferred annual contributions, the promoters of limited partnerships typically lowered their minimums to, what else, $2000.

Since most LPs are scheduled to run for ten years, it typically took a long time for those investors to realize the extent of their losses. But as *Financial World* reported in 1995, "Nothing has gone as promised for the 10,000,000 investors who were gulled into buying limited partnerships over the last twenty years."

Limited partnerships are a special form of business organization. The promoters of an LP become the general partner in the business, and investors are taken in as limited partners. Typically, the money raised from the investors is used as a down payment to purchase a product, perhaps jet aircraft, or oil rigs, or an apartment or office complex. The promoter promises the product will be leased out to end users for enough to pay all expenses, pay off the loans, and pay each limited partner a high annual income, typically 10 percent, usually for a period of ten years. At the end of the ten years, with the loans paid off, the promise is that the assets will be sold, easily providing enough cash so investing partners will get their original investment back, plus a healthy capital gain. Such a deal. Safety of capital. Ten years of high income. The return of the original investment, plus a capital gain.

The general partner customarily depends on brokerage firms, financial planners, personal business managers, anyone with access to individual investors, to bring in the limited partners. The middlemen are attracted by the very high commissions and upfront fees the general partner is willing to pay for the sale of the limited partnership "units" or "participations." *Studies show that in a typical LP, 20 to 25 percent of the investors' investment is used to pay upfront commissions and fees to those who bring the investors in, and the upfront fees and expenses of the general partner.* Therein lies the first problem. Only 75 to 80 percent of investors' money is left to actually invest in the project, putting the investment substantially in the hole before it gets off the ground.

Two generalities can be made about limited partnerships:

1. They're usually set up to take advantage of whatever has become hot in the public's mind—the latest fad.
2. Neither the general partner nor the brokerage firm selling the LP typically need have much concern about whether the project will be successful or not. They receive their profits from commissions and fees before the project gets off the ground, and in the case of the general partner, from ongoing fees for operating the project, whether or not it shows a profit. Generally, only the limited partners, that is, the public investors, risk their money and must depend on the venture being successful for their profit.

Public investors have been treated to LPs for the purpose of buying and leasing out commercial jets, luxury yachts, apartment complexes, office buildings, storage facilities, shopping malls, railroad cars, for oil and gas exploration, gold mining, financing motion pictures and Broadway shows, breeding race horses, cattle feeding, ostrich farming, fish farming, even

South American blood banks. In very few have investors even received their investment back, let alone made a profit, and in many, the losses have been on the order of 80 to 100 percent.

If you take nothing else from this book, take this advice: when you hear the words, "limited partnership" become extremely skeptical of the promises that will follow.

PSST! WANNA BUY AN OIL RIG?

In the 1980s, the media was filled with stories of a boom in wildcat oil and gas drilling. Fortunes were being made by independent drillers as well as established companies. The frenzied activity resulted in a shortage of drilling rigs. Sharp operators, mostly brokerage firms, jumped in, setting up limited partnerships for the purpose of buying new oil rigs that would be leased out to the exploration companies. Investors poured hundreds of millions of dollars into these plans. The story was irresistible. The sales brochures were full of dreams and promises. Suddenly, it seemed that every dentist just had to own a piece of an oil rig.

However, the LPs got started just as an oil and gas glut, created by an economic slowdown and the surge in drilling, caused oil and gas prices to plunge, making new drilling unprofitable. Demand for existing rigs plummeted. There was certainly no need for new rigs. Investors in oil rig LPs wound up owning thousands of new and expensive oil rigs, rusting in storage areas, unleased, with huge loans still due, and their value dropping like stones. Banks foreclosed, and the LPs were worthless disasters.

Interestingly, ten years later, with oil exploration beginning to pick up again, speculators bought those rusting drilling rigs for literally pennies on the dollar, held onto them for a while, and made fortunes feeding them into the revitalized demand.

RAILCAR LEASING

During an economic expansion in the 1980s, reports swept through the media of a shortage of railroad freight cars. Smart promoters jumped on the opportunity. Limited partnerships were set up for the purpose of purchasing new railcars and leasing them to the desperate railroads, for years of promised high income to investors, followed at the end of ten years by the return of each limited partner's investment, plus capital gains from the sale of the railcars. The brokers went to work on the sales end of it, and for a while it seemed like every dentist in the country now had to own a piece of a railcar.

The outcome? Huge upfront profits for the promoters and brokers. Disaster for the limited partners.

What happened to the promises?

Prior to the introduction of the various railcar limited partnerships, approximately 60,000 new railcars were built each year as replacement for aging cars and to take care of growth. Investors poured into the railcar idea with such enthusiasm that when all those LPs began ordering new railcars, the orders overwhelmed manufacturers to such an extent they had to build new plants to increase their production capacity. When the government finally stepped in to halt the sale of railcar LPs, there were 400,000 *excess* new railcars—a seven-year supply—sitting idle, rusting and unleased on railway sidings. The LPs owned those cars, for which there was no demand, but for which they still owed huge bank loans. The partnerships defaulted on the loans, the assets were seized by creditors, and the LPs were worthless. Twelve years later, that glut of railcars was still having an effect on the sale of railcars, with excess factory capacity still closed down.

REAL ESTATE LPS

Over the years, limited partnerships set up to purchase and lease out real estate have been among the most popular and easiest to sell LPs. Full-color brochures full of impressive pictures of shopping centers, high-rise office buildings, golf courses, or apartment complexes are striking. They certainly have coffee table appeal for those with a penchant for offhand remarks like, "Oh that? Yeah, I'm a partner in the deal."

Paine Webber, the nation's fourth largest brokerage firm, sold $2 billion worth of aircraft leasing, energy, and real estate LPs between 1980 and 1992. The sales pitch was one of capital preservation and safety. For instance, the Paine Webber/Pegasus (aircraft leasing) LPs, and Paine Webber/Geodyne (oil and gas) LPs promised immediate annual cash distributions of 12 percent, and according to Paine Webber internal documents, were sold to investors seeking income and capital preservation.

Yet, the partnerships turned out to be disasters for investors.

However, it took some years before investors realized the magnitude of their losses. Like most brokerage firms, Paine Webber continued to list the value of the LPs on investors' statements at the price the investor paid rather than at market value. As time went by, even though investors realized they weren't getting the promised annual income, they were not unduly alarmed as long as their $10,000 investment was shown on their statements as still being worth $10,000. It was not until the SEC disallowed the practice of showing LPs at "face value" and firms were required to show them at true market value, that investors realized the depth of their losses. The LPs had lost up to 70 percent of their value.

Lawsuits began to pileup against Paine Webber and virtually all major brokerage firms.

So what? Investing involves risk.

True. Investors have no right to expect the government or laws to protect them from investment risk. The only right they have is access to accurate information that is not presented in a fraudulent or deceptive manner.

Did the brokerage firms pass that test in their sales of limited partnerships?

A SAMPLING OF THE LAWSUITS

Paine Webber brokers were accused of making false statements and omitting material facts concerning risks, benefits, and suitability of the firm's LPs. Evidence mounted that the firm provided its brokers with special bonuses and deceptive sales scripts to help them push its LPs. For instance, in a 1990 sales script, brokers were told to close their sales pitch for Geodyne LPs by saying, "So Mr. _____, with the combination of high cash flow *and protection of your portfolio*, I believe a $15,000 investment in Geodyne today is smart. Do you agree with me that this is a wise move?"

Four law firms representing investors in Georgia, Florida, and Texas told the court that:

> The Paine Webber/Geodyne oil and gas LPs were sold on projections that investors would receive an income of 12 percent annually, even if oil and gas prices remained flat, when in fact the LP bought properties with the investors' money that it knew would produce losses for investors if oil and gas prices did not go up.

Internal documents from Paine Webber were presented that clearly showed the firm urged its brokers to sell these LPs to investors seeking low risk. As mentioned, in 1996, Paine Webber agreed to pay $292 million to settle SEC charges of fraud and misleading sales practices related to the sale of almost all the oil and gas, aircraft leasing, and real estate LPs the firm had sold between 1986 and 1992.

THE PRUDENTIAL SUITS

In pretrial hearings, Prudential admitted that to help them pitch its VMS Realty partnerships, it provided its brokers with a sales script that read in part, "Mr. _____, all you are doing is lending money to a major company that will borrow at established rates, give you a minimum of 12 percent per year for approximately 27 months, then give you a share of upside in real estate that they own or are developing. How much would you like in your account?" No mention that it was an investment with considerable downside risk. The brokers were told to make this pitch to "savers" who had their money in CDs and were probably dissatisfied with the interest rates they were receiving on those CDs. More disgusting, Prudential admitted it had its brokers continue to push the VMS partnerships even after learning that the income on the partnership's properties would not even cover paying the loans against the properties, let alone expenses, and income to investors. VMS Realty Partners participations later turned out to be all but worthless.

Some of the phrases in sales scripts Prudential provided its brokers for the sale of its LPs might sound familiar to readers:

"Piling up big bucks is the name of the game, and have I got a game for you!"

"REMEMBER, the general partner is Prudential—solid as a rock!"

"Prudential is the largest private owner of real estate in the world. Without question the strongest general partner in existence. Get a piece of the rock!"

"The investment goal is low risk and safety!"

As mentioned, Prudential was also allowed to settle the charges out of court. The settlement required Prudential to admit criminal wrongdoing and pay partial restitution to cheated customers who made a claim. However, it was agreed that Prudential would not be indicted on the criminal charges unless it was caught committing similar crimes within three years. Honest. That's exactly what it said. Can you imagine an individual stealing billions of dollars and being told that if he or she will give some of it back, and is not caught doing anything similar for three years, he or she won't be prosecuted? Hell, no. We see unemployed persons given three-year prison sentences for stealing shoes for their kids.

Prudential's restitution fund was the largest ever imposed on a brokerage firm, surpassing the $650 million in fines paid by Drexel Burham Lambert as a result of its 1988 guilty plea admitting securities and mail fraud.

Frankly, we could fill a volume or two on the subject, but these few examples should suffice to indicate that not much has changed in the brokerage industry in its *attitude* toward public investors since regulations were introduced in 1933.

CHAPTER 17

PSST! WHAT LOOKS GOOD?

INVESTORS ARE ALSO STILL FREE TO BE FOOLISH

Many investors have the notion that they are responsible for small losses they may suffer, but that the regulations are in place to protect them from large losses.

That thought is demonstrated by the surge in claims against brokerage firms that usually takes place after bear markets, the most common complaint being that particular investments were "unsuitable" and the risk was not explained. Worried in recent years about a similar legal avalanche after the next bear market, a number of brokerage firms set up "early intervention units" to deal with claims before they reach the legal system. Joel Leifer, a New York attorney that represents brokerage firms, reported that even after the market's brief stumble in 1998, one firm's early intervention unit saw claims rise 40 percent above normal.

The "I should be protected from my mistakes" attitude may be partially due to misunderstanding brokerage firm advertising such as "accounts are insured for up to $500,000." However, such insurance is not designed to protect investors from investment losses, only from losses they would suffer if the brokerage firm went bankrupt, closed up, or otherwise could not or would not return the investor's assets.

Protecting investors against investment losses would simply not make sense in a free market system. The mission statement of the SEC makes that very clear. It states that SEC oversight is based on the principle that investing involves risk, and it is not the government's role, responsibility, or intention, to alleviate that risk, nor is it the government's role to protect investors from their own foolishness.

The goal of regulations *is* to provide a level playing field, by preventing the dissemination of false and misleading investment information, to make all information available to everyone at the same time, and to prevent those who must have the information first from trading on it before it is made public.

However, it's one thing to make information available, quite another to get investors to seek it out or use it. It's not a new problem.

In the early part of the century, there were few sources of independent research on stocks. Investment advisory newsletters were put out primarily by brokerage firms themselves, who used them as "business getters," as Richard D. Wyckoff, a brokerage firm partner at the time, put it. Toward the end of his career, Wyckoff, aware that public investors desperately needed to know how the markets really worked, and needed a source of stock recommendations from independent research rather than from brokerage firms, decided to publish an independent newsletter. "There was nothing like it at the time," he said.

He assumed the public would clamor for such information, and introduced a monthly newsletter, *The Ticker*, for which he charged $3 per year. It quickly became a success in providing excellent stock research and recommendations, and was sought out by market professionals. It was also a critical success in providing sound information on how the market really operated. But no matter how hard he tried, he could not get enough subscriptions from the public to meet his expenses.

After several years, he re-evaluated the situation:

I had for the first time in my life run into debt, attempting to teach the public how to play the market, only to find out they didn't want to learn. I could tell from their letters that all they wanted was to be told what to buy or sell. So, I decided to give them what they wanted, and announced a weekly tip sheet, The Trend Letter. My publishing problems were over. Subscriptions poured in. They were willing to pay more in a month for this than I had asked for a year of the other. The price of the one page mimeographed Trend Letter was $50 a year. It could have been done with pen and ink on wrapping paper, as long as it only provided the stock tips.

There has been no change in that peculiarity of investors to be interested only in hot tips in modern times.

The most popular features on TV financial news shows are the buy, sell, or hold segments, and brief interviews with money managers or analysts who give quick one-sentence assessments of a half dozen stocks in two minutes. The most popular sections of financial magazines are the quick tables of 20-20 hindsight that rank the top-performing mutual funds of the most recent period, with little regard to how the performance was achieved, or whether it is likely to continue in the future. The most popular investment advisory newsletters? Digests that contain thumbnail abstracts of the stock picks of dozens of original research newsletters.

Another indication: there are more than 40 million investors in the United States. Yet publications like *Barron's, The Wall Street Journal*, and *Investors' Business Daily* have subscriber bases that range from only 400,000 to 2 million, and most of those subscribers are probably professionals since there are 550,000 stockbrokers alone in the United States, and as many or more bankers, money managers, and corporate chiefs. Fewer than 5 percent of individual investors seem to have more than superficial interest in the workings of the market where their life savings are at risk.

INVESTIGATE THOSE TIPS

If you're going to invest on tips, at least investigate the tips before committing your money. The stocks will still be there the next day, and the next week, and will probably even be cheaper once the initial bounce from the publicized tip wears off. Keep in mind you're not exactly receiving one-on-one information. There are up to a million other people receiving the tip at the same time.

Look at it this way. If you were interested in that dough-nut shop we were talking about earlier, you wouldn't write out a check for it on the spot, sight unseen, at the asking price, based on a real estate broker calling to let you know it was available, and relying solely on the broker's pitch that it's a great business. You would look into the situation quite thor-oughly, and would probably bring in an accountant and an attorney to also look things over to make sure the situation is as the seller, and the broker, say it is. That would not be a reflection on your opinion of the real estate broker, but just a commonsense realization that those who depend on commis-sions for a living have personal pressures, like putting food on the table and making the mortgage payment, that may carry a higher priority than concern about your success in the dough-nut business.

It's not possible to look *that* thoroughly into an investment in a publicly traded company. You're certainly not going to spend hours touring their facilities, going through file cabinets, asking probing questions of the president and treasurer, and poring over the financial statements. But you need to do more than write out the check sight unseen.

Yet investors will plunk down $25,000 on a stock tip with less investigation than they would apply to the selection of a $500 TV set, even though the disparity between different stocks is far greater than that between different brands of TVs.

The failure to check out tips sometimes becomes almost hilarious.

I spoke not too long ago with a woman who was making great profits from 500 shares of Intel she had owned for quite some time. She thought she had bought into a company that had "something to do with international telephone service."

Another person talked to me about owning 100 shares of HBO because someone had tipped him off that it was a very profitable company. He said it sounded good to him because they had the best movies of all the cable channels. I didn't have the heart to tell him that what he owned was HBO & Co., the large health-care information services company, a great company and a great stock, but not the TV movie channel (which is a wholly owned subsidiary of Time-Warner).

When Prohibition was about to be repealed, the stocks of companies that made supplies for the soon-to-be-legal liquor industry became valid hot stocks. Owens Illinois Glass Company, the bottle manufacturer, was such a stock. Another entirely different company, Libby Owens Ford Glass Company, made plate glass, mostly for the automobile industry, and had nothing whatever to gain from the repeal of Prohibition. However, Joseph Kennedy and Walter Chrysler figured the company names were similar enough that the public could be duped into confusing them. So, they formed a pool and bought call options on 65,000 shares of Libby Owens Ford Glass. Sure enough, they soon had the public confused, and their glass company's stock soared right along with the other.

A couple of years ago, TCI Communications, the huge cable company, became the subject of excited merger talk. The company's stock traded on the NASDAQ under the symbol TCOM, and it started to soar. At the same time, an entirely different company, Transcontinental Realty Inc., trading on the NYSE under the symbol TCI, saw its stock soar on four times its normal volume. The company's management was dumbfounded until someone discovered investors were piling into the stock thinking it was the cable company everyone was so excited about.

How little investigation would be required to at least confirm the name, ticker symbol, and business of the company being purchased?

Investigation is important no matter how impressive the source of a stock recommendation might be.

CERTIFIED BLUE-RIBBON TIPS ARE NOT EXEMPT

A few years ago, in 1992, the American Stock Exchange announced a significant effort to assist investors in choosing good stocks. It introduced what it called its Emerging Company Marketplace. A "blue-ribbon" screening panel appointed by the exchange would periodically choose and announce "the champagne of promising small growth companies." What better place for investors, searching for the next WalMart or Microsoft, to shop?

Hundreds of red, white, and blue balloons floated down to the trading floor to the cheers of floor brokers, as exchange officials announced the first group of those exciting blue-ribbon companies. Public investors poured into the stocks for weeks after their names were released.

A look at the performance of the exchange's champagne of small growth companies two years later, in 1994, however, was a view of disillusioned investors. Of the sixty companies that had been touted, only a handful were still worth what investors paid for them. The majority, 66 percent, had declined in value. A number had been delisted, no longer trading at all. Among those that still traded, many of the losses were awful:

Advanced Photonix	-73%
American Pacific Mint	-48%
Audre Recognition Systems	-81%
Cancer Treatment Holdings	-55%
Epigen	-84%
Ion Laser Technology	-68%
Media Logic	-44%
Medphone	-99%
North Coast Energy	-47%
Ocean Optique Distributors	-42%
Printon	-98%
Professional Dental Tech	-39%
Randers Group	-61%

During the same period, the Russell 2000 Index of 2000 small stocks *gained* 23 percent.

As Gary Weis and Michael Schroeder said in a 1994 *Business Week* article,

> Retail investors made the mistake of thinking the American Stock Exchange's list of Emerging Company Marketplace companies was a conglomeration of the best companies in the country. That was a tall order. But, if companies promoted on the ECM can't be among the best in America, is it too much to ask that they not be among the worst?

In its "analysis" of companies for inclusion in this elite group, the exchange's blue-ribbon panel even missed the fact that one of its final group, Printon Inc., had as its chairman and CEO a person who had twice been sued by the SEC, accused of defrauding investors.

What could an investor have done rather than simply jump on the name as soon as it was released?

Well, what would the investor do if he or she were investing in a TV set or an automobile? The investor would listen to the salesperson's pitch, no doubt learning things he or she hadn't known or considered. Then, the investor would probably gather information on several competing brands, pick up a brochure on each, and read about and compare the specifications and features. The investor might get a copy of a consumer test report. He or she might ask friends or relatives about their experiences with similar brands. Above all, the investor would mull the idea over for a while, maybe just overnight, more likely for at least several days. In the end, the investor would reach a decision to buy or not to buy. Even after deciding to buy, he or she would likely shop around or negotiate for the best possible price.

A similar approach to the more important decision about whether or not to buy a stock should begin with at least obtaining a research report on the company.

BROKERAGE FIRM RESEARCH

If the recommendation is coming from a full-service broker, it's a simple matter to ask for the research report from which the broker is quoting. The broker is quite likely telling you only the positive side of the picture and may even be embellishing it to a significant degree. However, the research departments of most brokerage firms put out research for their brokers and customers that is considerably more balanced than many investors realize. When investments go bad, and a percentage will, the firms certainly don't want their own written research to support claims that they provided only one side of the story. In fact, the research reports are frequently so careful in presenting the negatives that many brokers are reluctant to send out the full report. You may have to be insistent if they make excuses, and downright suspicious if you receive only photocopies of selected pages.

This might be a good place to mention an obvious fact, but one that's frequently overlooked in the excitement of receiving a stock tip on a great potential winner: for every buyer, there has to be a seller. Otherwise, the trade couldn't take place. So keep in mind that for every person who has researched a company and made an intelligent decision that it's a good stock to buy, there has to be a seller who has reached the opposite conclusion. That realization alone should prompt you every time to want to know the negatives of the situation before you make a decision.

It's more difficult to get comprehensive research from discount brokers. Some of the larger ones have begun to provide limited research. Most provide none at all.

RESEARCH DIRECT FROM THE COMPANY

Most companies will gladly provide considerable information on their operations, including annual reports, quarterly financial statements, and copies of their most recent filings with the SEC.

INDEPENDENT RESEARCH

Research reports on virtually all companies are available for a fee from sources like *Dow Jones News/Retrieval* and *Dun & Bradstreet.*

The Value Line Investment Survey provides concise one-page snapshots of 1700 companies, positives and negatives, updating their profiles every quarter.

Independent "original research" newsletters include research reports for their subscribers on the specific stocks they are recommending at any given time, but not on stock tips you've picked up elsewhere.

A number of newsletters compile the activity of company insiders. It's always wise to know whether a company's insiders are buying or selling its stocks, as long as you realize there are often reasons to do so that are unrelated to the stock's prospects.

DON'T FOOL YOURSELF

As an investor, you've got enough people trying to fool you. Don't also fool yourself. If you've received a stock recommendation from whatever source, and then find two or three different Internet chat rooms, or tip sites, where the exciting prospects of the same stock are being touted, that is not helpful research, or corroboration of the validity of the recommendation. If you notice spokespeople from several brokerage firms or mutual funds traveling the financial talk shows, touting the same stocks, that is not corroborative research. What you need is the full story, including the negatives, so you can make a judgment.

Think of it this way. If you're shopping for a house, by the time you've tentatively settled on one you really want you're already aware of its positives. But you know there must be some hidden negatives since there are negatives to some degree in every situation. You don't want to discover when it's too late that the negatives outweigh the positives, and if you had known about them you wouldn't have made the purchase. So, you primarily look under the sinks and poke around the basement, *looking for* the negatives.

Investing in a stock, you want to know if the company's new medical product has exciting potential, but two other companies are coming out with competing products, or that the Internet company's sales are indeed growing exponentially, but profits are unlikely for three years. These may not be negatives that overcome the positives, but at least you will have the full story and will know whether your tipster was telling you the full story. You will also know what to be watchful for as time passes. Knowing that profits are unlikely for three years, you will know to become even more excited when the company shows a small profit just six months later.

DON'T PUT YOUR FUTURE ON A ROULETTE WHEEL

If you're going to have important money in the stock market—money expected to grow for a comfortable retirement, college educations, a better lifestyle—and you're going to manage that money yourself, you really need to learn as much about the business of money and risk management, and about the markets, as you can. You would not undertake much simpler do-it-yourself projects where harm can come, such as wiring your home, doing your own taxes, or even doing your own plumbing or carpenter work, without learning as much as you can about how professionals handle the work.

CHAPTER 18

OF MERMAIDS AND LEPRECHAUNS

DISPENSING WITH THE MYTHS OF WALL STREET

It's the myths that surround investing that are the biggest obstacles to investors understanding, preparing for, and benefiting from bear markets. We've covered some of them in detail:

- The fantasy that the stock market is just a fuzzy, cuddly, easy money machine
- The myth that good stocks will hold up in market declines
- The fantasy that buy and hold investing is the way to go for public investors
- The illusion that professionals, insiders, and institutions are buy and hold investors
- The myth that bears are either extinct or toothless
- The lie that public investors aren't smart enough to engage in market timing and risk management

Let's look quickly at a few other myths that pertain not so much to staying on the right side of the market cycles, but are myths that can affect investing performance any time.

WE STILL GET ONLY WHAT WE PAY FOR

We mentioned discount brokers earlier. Let's return to that subject for a moment. From 1790 to 1975, all brokerage firms charged the same fixed commissions for all customers, retail or institutional. It was an absolute requirement if they were to retain trading privileges on the NYSE. It had become a requirement in the late 1700s when trading in stocks still took place in the street. There were some brokers, considered by others to be mavericks, who began selling stocks at lower prices and for lower commissions. The leading twenty-four merchant-brokers immediately banded together in an effort to end that kind of competition. On May 17, 1792, those leading brokers signed a historic document known as the Buttonwood Agreement, which would allow them to control the activity of Wall Street. The agreement was brief and to the point. They agreed:

- To buy or sell securities for their own inventories, and for their customers, only at their own auction
- Commissions would be maintained at a fixed rate
- Outsiders would not be permitted to attend
- All other upstart markets and auctions would be avoided and ignored

Those twenty-four controlling merchants soon moved the securities auction into a large room above the nearby Tontine Coffee House. On March 8, 1817, the members formalized a constitution establishing themselves as the New York Stock Exchange Board. The word "Board" was later dropped from the name.

From that day until April 30, 1975, the NYSE required that fixed commissions be charged by all member firms. But in 1975, 158 years after the Buttonwood Agreement, the SEC finally ordered the exchange to abolish fixed commissions. With that change to competitive pricing, the profile of brokerage firms began to change.

Discount brokerage firms came on the scene. By dispensing with research departments and portfolio management for investors, they were able to cut commissions in half and more.

That in turn pushed traditional brokerage firms to supplement their incomes by expansion into other financial products, including proprietary mutual funds, insurance, real estate, tax shelters, and limited partnerships.

In the meantime, discount brokerage firms became increasingly more aggressive. Fifty percent discounts became 60 percent discounts, then gave way to $30 a trade, $20, $15, $9 *round trip*. In the last few years, particularly with the introduction of trading by computer and on the Internet, has come scattered instances of *no-commission* trading.

What are investors thinking when they fall for this stuff? That one no-frills discount firm needs $60 per trade and the firm winds up with 10 percent profit at the end of the year, but another can stay in business at $9 per trade, and another by charging no commissions? It doesn't take much common sense to realize the customer is paying the firm's costs, plus a profit, in some other manner, usually in the way the customer's order is executed. Let's look at just one potential area. How many investors have ever heard of SEC Rule 19c-3?

The rule was suggested by the securities industry and issued in 1979. Since then, brokerage firms have been able to "internalize" trades, that is, execute the trades of many stocks within the firm, without taking the trade to the auction floor of an exchange for competitive pricing. The rule limits the size of such trades to 1000 shares or fewer, so it mostly affects public investors. Upon issuance of the rule change, most brokerage firms set up 19c-3 desks, and a significant number of small investor orders are executed at those desks because of the extra profit potential for the firm.

For instance, suppose a stock is quoted on the NYSE at 20¼ bid, 20½ asked. If the firm sends your order to the exchange floor for execution, the firm's floor broker will probably enter a bid between the spread, at 20³/₈, in an effort to get the customer the best possible price, and chances are the trade will be made at 20³/₈. However, if the firm executes the trade at its own 19c-3 desk, the operator of that desk does not even have to try to get the customer a better price. He or she can simply

execute the trade at 20½, the last asked price on the NYSE.
After filling the customer's order at that price, the operator can
then enter an order for the desk's own account "between the
spread" at 20³⁄₈. The firm keeps the extra ¹⁄₈ per share, perhaps
more, depending on how wide the spread is at the time.

"I do it all day," said the 19c-3 desk operator at one firm.
"An extra $125 on every 1000 shares traded, all day long.
Minting money. And the beauty of it is that it doesn't even
show up as commission on the customer's confirmation slip."

Under those circumstances, $20 per trade commissions,
$10 commissions, even zero commissions aren't such a bargain
after all.

FULL SERVICE OR DO IT YOURSELF

Investors should also consider whether they really are better off
with any discount broker, at the cost of giving up the full-service
broker's research department and watchful supervision of the
account. Investors see only the savings of a few dollars on the
trade commission. We've already mentioned the value of a full-
service firm's research department to investors, not just on stocks
the firm is recommending, but for stocks the investors have come
up with themselves but on which they need more information.
Also consider the advantage of follow-up service. Suppose news
comes out some months later on a stock an investor is holding.
The investor's full-service broker, with the stock "flagged" for
breaking news on his or her computer, is going to know instantly. Chances are it will be days before an investor using a discount
broker will hear the news. Such an investor's first indication that
something is wrong usually comes when he or she notices the
stock going down sharply for a number of days and begins to
search out the reason. If the stock has lost a few dollars a share
in the meantime, the few pennies a share the investor saved by
placing the trade with a discount broker is meaningless.

Investors also need to realize that almost any full-service
broker will provide them a discount on commissions simply for
the asking, allowing them to have the best of both worlds. But

you do have to ask! An automobile dealer isn't going to give you a better price if you don't ask, and neither will a stockbroker.

COMPUTERIZED TRADING—OR IS IT?

Another myth many investors believe is that because they have a computer and use it to place their trades overnight, they are somehow engaged in computerized trading, or at least the twenty-four hour trading they've heard that professionals use. Hardly. Professionals trade twenty-four hours a day by trading on Instinet, the computerized trading forum from which the public is pretty well excluded, and by trading on foreign markets in the hours when the U.S. market is closed.

The only thing public investors accomplish by sending their orders to their brokers overnight via computer is that they set their order in the queue for "market on open" pricing the following morning. Not always a good idea if news comes out before the open that drives the stock or the entire market significantly one way or the other. It's far more advisable to place orders only when the market is open and the stock is trading.

LUCKY INSIDERS IN THE MODERN MARKET

Are we now protected by regulations from the manipulative trading of corporate insiders, or is that also a myth? Trading on inside information, that is, information not yet available to the public, has been illegal since the introduction of regulations in 1933. However, we should be as lucky as insiders still seem to be.

There have been thousands of examples of their luck over the years. Just for fun, we'll look at a couple of them.

In 1995, Horizon Healthcare became a popular stock when it acquired Continental Medical Systems, becoming Horizon/CMS. The stock climbed to $28 per share by March 1996. Unfortunately, at that point, the company made a series of announcements about problems that were negatively affecting earnings. The stock plunged 24 percent in one day, and within four weeks, had dropped 50 percent. It was interesting that a month or so later, *The Wall Street Journal* learned from filings with the SEC that Horizon/CMS insiders, including the company's chairman and CEO, had unloaded $37 million of stock at the highs just a few weeks before the negative announcements were made. It must have been just a lucky coincidence since the insiders said that at the time they sold they were unaware of the problems they'd be announcing a few weeks later.

Insiders at Circuit City ran into similar luck. Circuit City stock had climbed 35 percent in the early months of 1996, but then plunged in mid-April when the company announced April sales were running lower than expected. Later SEC filings showed that nine insiders, including senior executives and members of the board of directors, sold a combined 185,000 shares between April 8 and April 12, just days before the negative announcement was made. Questioned, the company said its insiders had sold "for personal reasons," were unaware of the disappointing sales that would be announced a few days later, and had no reason to *expect* a drop in the stock. Such good luck.

The newsletter *The Insiders*, mentioned earlier, makes an occasional tongue-in-cheek "Lucky Insider" award. One recipient in 1997 was American Residential Services, which trades on the NYSE. *The Insiders* quotes the company's president saying on September 3, "We continue to be pleased with the success of our strategy. . . . The company's commercial services margins are stronger than expected." The following *day*, September 4, he sold 10 percent of his stock in the company, and over the next two days, the company's CFO unloaded 10,000 shares, and a senior vice president sold 33 percent of his holdings. On September 23, less than three weeks later, the company's president announced that things weren't going so well, and earnings were not going to meet analysts' estimates! Of course, they didn't trade on inside information not available to the public, but what luck that they had sold three weeks earlier. With the negative earnings announcement, the stock plunged 50 percent in less than a month.

PUBLICIZING STOCKS IN THE MODERN MARKET

We also don't have to worry about misleading publicity being used to harmfully manipulate the public in or out of stocks like in the old days. Regulations introduced after the 1929 stock market crash also made that activity illegal. Therefore, when we see mutual fund and brokerage firm spokespeople leaving their businesses to travel the interview circuit, enthusiastically recommending stocks they have in their portfolios, we need not be suspicious. They can't be doing so to bring more public buying to their stocks to drive their profits higher, and certainly not to boost public demand so they can unload their holdings into the demand. We can know they're going to all that effort solely out of a strong desire to make total strangers wealthy.

Once in a while, the publicity does look suspicious and is mentioned in the media. Once in a greater while, the SEC will investigate, but no abuses are discovered.

For example, in 1995, Jeffrey Vinik, manager at the time of Fidelity's Magellan Fund, touted Micron Technology in magazine interviews. It was discovered later that at the same time public investors were reading of those recommendations, Vinik's fund was engaged in significant selling of Micron stock. After *The Wall Street Journal* and others discovered and reported the activity, the SEC launched an investigation, saying the behavior "raises questions" under provisions of the 1934 Securities Act that govern market manipulation.

However, it concluded the investigation in 1996, saying that there was no evidence of an attempt to hold the prices up on Micron while the Magellan Fund unloaded its holdings. It was just that, by coincidence, Vinik changed his mind about the stock between the time he gave the interviews and when the magazines hit the newsstands, and so began selling it. A very lucky coincidence they might have added, considering what happened to the stock after the fund unloaded its holdings in it. Lucky for the fund that is, not so lucky for any public investors that piled into the stock as a result of Vinik's interviews. Micron stock plunged 75 percent from mid-1995 to mid-1996.

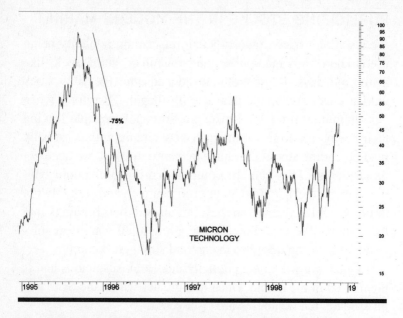

-75%

MICRON
TECHNOLOGY

1995   1996   1997   1998   19

MICRON TECHNOLOGY PLUNGED 75 PERCENT FROM ITS 1995 HIGH TO ITS 1996 LOW.

WATCH THOSE PERFORMANCE CLAIMS

Performance claims can also have a mythical quality to them. For example, a money manager or fund manager who begins with $100,000 in assets under management and makes $100,000 the first year, can accurately claim he or she was up 100 percent on the year. If that performance then brings in more money and the manager has $10,000,000 under management for the second year, but loses $5,000,000 and so is down 50 percent for the second year, under current industry standards the manager can announce his or her two-year rate of return averaged + 25 percent. That's a far stretch from the fact that over the two years the money manager lost $4,950,000 of the $10,000,000 placed in his or her care.

A few years ago, an investment newsletter attracted the attention of the SEC when it sent out a direct-mail piece claiming across its front page that its recommendations would have turned $10,000 into several billions over a ten-year period.

I suspect nothing was ever heard from that investigation because the newsletter publisher had covered himself by explaining in fine print on the inside that the claim was based on an assumption that an investor would use 50X leverage in following the recommendations. The author did not explain how an investor could get that kind of leverage, when buying on maximum 50 percent margin produces only 2X leverage. The bottom line was that by backing out the supposed 50X annual leverage, the service's recommendations had averaged a gain of *less than 10 percent per year* for the ten years.

Another interesting method of advertising is a statement such as, "If you had invested in just 6 of our recommended stocks last year you would have made an average profit of 60 percent." What they don't tell you is that they made 200 recommendations, of which the six best gained an average of 60 percent. The other 194 recommendations could have given you losses of 100 percent for all the information the ad tells you.

BROKERAGE FIRM PERFORMANCE

Here's an angle on performance that will surprise many readers, and tells quite a story by itself. When your broker tells you he or she just won a performance award for the month, or for the quarter, I bet you assume your broker is talking about profit performance for his or her customers. At least that's what I always thought. What other kind of performance could possibly be important? It was quite a surprise to find out that brokerage firms don't even calculate or rank their broker's performance regarding making profits for customers. The performance that is measured, and for which awards and bonuses are paid, is whether sales quotas are met or exceeded, and the degree to which a broker manages to bring money into the firm's highest profit areas such as its proprietary mutual funds, wrap accounts, and limited partnerships.

MYTHS THAT WON'T DIE

In early chapters, we spoke of how the market is like a river that carries virtually all stocks with it, in either direction, and why even good stocks plunge in bear markets. Yet, well-meaning analysts go to great lengths to help investors find safe-haven stocks for pending market declines. The most popular include food, beverage, and drug stocks, on the theory that even when the stock market is down people still have to eat, drink, and take their medicines. The theory completely ignores the fact that, as explained earlier, it doesn't matter if a company's sales and earnings hold up or even continue to grow during a market decline. If its stock is selling at a high multiple of the company's earnings, the stock will still plunge once investors are no longer willing to pay those high multiples.

Another myth that pops up every once in a while in troublesome market times is that stocks that pay high dividends will hold up well in a bear market. The theory is that investors will continue to hold them and even buy more because the dividend income offsets the losses that might be seen from a decline in the stock price. Amid the 1998 correction, a very highly regarded financial publication published a well-meaning article in which it told its readers that high-dividend stocks with good earnings records would be "life preservers" in a bear market because the extra value of the dividend "would help keep the stock afloat in turbulent seas." The article then went on to list the fifty best candidates it had come up with through a computerized search. Just for fun, I checked how they had performed in the 1987 crash. The top ten stocks on the list declined an average of 41.3 percent in a bear market in which the Dow declined only 36.1 percent. The publication graciously printed my letter pointing that out to them, including my comment that a sinking investor might as well be thrown an anchor as such "life preserver" stocks.

Myths die hard, and mostly not at all.

CHAPTER 19

BEAR MARKETS ALSO END

Let's get back to good news—in fact, very good news.

Bull markets have an easy task convincing investors they'll never end. But they do. Bear markets have an equally easy task convincing investors that *they* will never end. But they also do.

When bear markets do end, investors are presented with a buying opportunity seen only once in a great while. Since the next bear market *we* see is likely to be the most severe the market has suffered since 1929, it follows that the subsequent buying opportunity, at the bear market low, is likely to be the best buying opportunity of current investors' lifetimes.

Not when the market is more overvalued than it has ever been in history, but *then*, will be the time for investors to clean out their savings, borrow against insurance policies, take out a second mortgage on the family home, and even move the kids' college money into the stock market. *Then*, not at a time when the market is more overbought than it has ever been in history, will be the time to buy on margin. Not when everyone from high school investment groups to grandmothers' knitting circles is euphoric about the stock market, but *then*, when the last determined buy and hold investor of the 1990's bull market has bailed out and has no interest in the market, will be the time. Not now, when Microsoft and General Electric are selling at fifty-three and thirty-three times earnings, but *then*, when many similar great

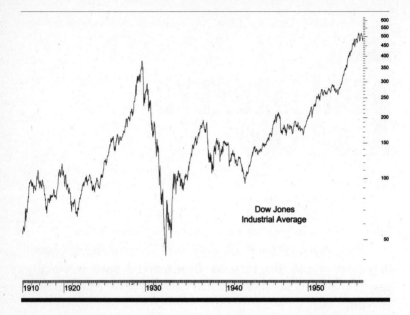

Dow Jones
Industrial Average

companies will be selling at less than ten times earnings, will be the time. Not now, when evidence points to corporations and Wall Street institutions unloading their high-priced stocks into the public's careless enthusiasm (while encouraging the public to hang tough with a buy and hold strategy), but *then*, when that same so-called smart money will be loading up again at the bargain prices (while telling public investors it's not yet time).

By putting ourselves enthusiastically on the buy side of the market, not near the top of a bull market, but when stocks are on the low-risk bargain tables, we can truly harness the power of the stock market that makes it the best investing vehicle of all.

Let's look at that granddaddy of them all, the 1929–1932 bear market, from a different view—not from the perspective of the damage it caused, but from the perspective of the opportunity it provided for making fortunes. Remember how Kennedy and Baruch and Danforth made millions in the decline, not by holding good stocks that they bought near the top, but by selling even good stocks short?

Did they sell short at the exact top? Did they even know for sure when the top arrived? Definitely not. Kennedy's friends, and particularly his enemies, ribbed him unmercifully when he sold every stock he owned when the market stumbled in early 1929, thinking the top was in, only to have the market resume its euphoric ways. His associates urged him to get back in, but he refused, saying, "Only a fool holds out for top dollar." He then watched with growing fascination as the market spiked up in its final blow-off top in 1929. He observed that even his cab drivers and waiters were giving him stock tips, and that as a measure of the mania that was driving everything up, they were invariably right in their picks.

When the top did arrive, few recognized it or believed it. There had been a number of "warning shots across the bow," when corrections took place and some sold out believing this was it, only to have the market resume its upward enthusiasm, and they scrambled back in. After several such whipsaws, even those who usually knew better, became convinced that this time was somehow different. That created the tragedy of the 1929–1932 bear market. Normally, Wall Street operators and institutions would have sold into the public's final excitement. They would have had the cash to buy when "fair market" values were reached, and perhaps the decline in the bear market would have been of the 50 percent variety, serious enough to wipe out buy and hold investors, particularly those who bought on margin or with other borrowed money, but not enough to destroy the entire economy and the country.

But, in the late 1920s, even Wall Street became a believer of its own hype, that "this time is different," and so eventually got caught in the downdraft. When the market got down to levels that would normally have been fair value levels, not even they had the cash to buy and, in fact, were still trying to bail out. And thus, that bear market continued down to more extreme levels of undervalue than had ever been seen. Even brokers, bankers, and corporate heads were bankrupted by the crash and, not used to handling adversity, jumped from office windows and shot themselves at their country estates. The rest of the country went on to endure the years of bread lines, bank closings, and 20 percent unemployment of the Great Depression.

However, look at that chart again, and imagine the opportunity for those few who had recognized the risk near the top, curbed their greed, sold out, and had cash at the 1932 low. Although previous buy and hold investors might have been saying, "If I hadn't lost everything, I'd certainly be buying now," there were obviously some who were able to buy since the market took off like a rocket.

The gain over the next five years, to the 1937 high, was 468 percent. An investor who took $100,000 out of the market anywhere near its peak would have turned it into $468,000 over those five years. A buy and hold investor with $100,000 in the market at the peak would have had $14,000 left at the 1932 bottom, and that 468 percent rise in the next bull market would have brought his or her portfolio back up to only $65,500. At that point another bear market, with a 50 percent decline, took place, and the $65,500 would have been back down to $32,750. It was not until 1954 that a buy and hold investor would have seen his or her portfolio back even to its 1929 level of $100,000.

A bear market invariably wipes out several, even many, years of previous gains and the recovery back to previous highs takes a long time, an interminably long time if you're waiting with all of your assets in the market watching their value disappear month by endless month, year after endless year.

However, the length of time that market timers wait for a bear market to end and present the next buying opportunity is not usually a long time at all. In that worst ever 1929–1932 bear market, it took the market twenty-five years to get back to its 1929 level, but only three years for the bottom to be in and for the next spectacular buying opportunity to present itself.

Let's look at the chart of another bear market, that of 1973–1974, not from the perspective of its damage, but from the perspective of the buying opportunity it presented.

The bear market wiped out 45 percent of the market's value in two years and, not shown on the chart, *wiped out the previous fourteen years of market gains*. Think about that for a moment. A buy and hold investor who had courageously held through the

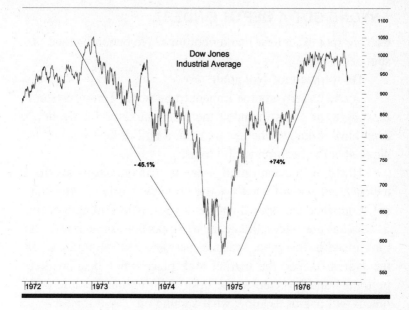

pain of the four bear markets that had taken place between 1961 and 1973, as cataloged in the table in Chapter 1, saw all the gains from those pains wiped out anyway, when this 1973–1974 bear market plunged the market back to its 1959 level.

Note also in the chart how several rally attempts (mostly during the favorable seasonal periods), kept buy and hold investors tucked right in there fully invested, and probably buying the dips at Wall Street's insistence if they were not fully invested.

However, look at what happened to the portfolios of those who took their profits in 1972, and had all of their cash to invest when undervalued levels were reached at or near the bear market low. The next buying opportunity, at the bear market low, arrived in less than two years, two years, we hope, in which they made further gains from the downside. In any event, the next buying opportunity was soon upon them, and they made an *additional* 74 percent in a year and a half in the next bull market, while buy and hold investors needed that entire bull market just to get back to even.

ANYONE GOT A DEPTH FINDER?

Can we spot exact bear market bottoms? No better than we can spot exact tops.

Do we need to? Not at all.

We've already got the Enhanced Seasonal Timing System. Its long-term gains included the bear markets. So, we don't even have to know whether we're in a bull or bear market, let alone spot the bear market bottoms.

However, we don't really want to manage our assets from a closet, unaware of what's going on in the world and the market. And since our drawdowns in the Seasonal Timing System, as small as they were, did occur when portions of bear markets took place in favorable seasonal periods, and the times when the system lagged the market took place when bear markets bottomed and reversed to the upside during unfavorable periods, it will pay us to know what's going on.

Just as we are not able to determine the exact top of a bull market, but can quite easily tell when risk becomes very high, and so prepare for a top as a bull market matures, we are also unable to determine the exact bottom of a bear market, but can quite easily tell when market risk has become very low, indicating that a bear market is approaching its end game.

HOW CLOSE NEED WE COME?

Contrary to popular opinion, close enough doesn't count only in horse shoes and hand grenades. It also makes you a winner in the stock market. Just as it doesn't matter if we get all the tail end of a bull market because those gains will be given back in the subsequent bear market, so it doesn't matter if we get in too early or too late at the bear market bottom. Just as long as we get in when risk is low so that odds are high, the subsequent bull market will surge higher than our entry point.

Let's use another chart to demonstrate.

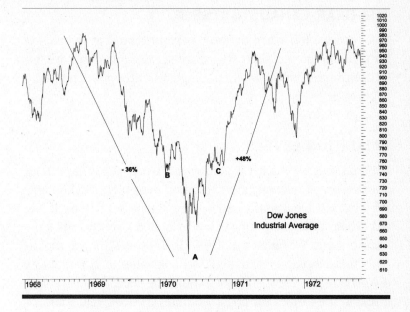

This chart looks almost identical to the last one that showed the 1973–1974 bear market. But as we already know, the long-term pattern is for a bear market to come along on average every 3.3 years. This chart is of the 1968–1970 bear market.

The point of the chart is to indicate that, just as it's not necessary to identify the exact top of a bull market since the subsequent bear market will wipe out that gain and much more, so it's not necessary to identify the exact bottom of a bear market.

In the preceding chart, if we managed to reenter exactly at the low at A, we would have enjoyed a spectacular 48 percent gain over the next twelve months. However, even if we entered either three months earlier at B or not until the fall of 1970, at C, *or anytime between B and C*, we still would have enjoyed an excellent 27 percent gain over the following twelve months. On a buy and hold basis, the market did not even get back to its 1968 peak in that next bull market. In fact, the market didn't get to exceed its 1968 peak (985 on the Dow) in a meaningful way until it finally managed to break out above 1000, twelve years later in 1982.

THE BEAR EXHAUSTS ITSELF

How can we tell when the bear is getting tired of rampaging through the campground? By using the same guidelines we use to determine a bull market is at high risk of topping out, only in reverse.

VALUATION LEVELS

Obviously, if the market is at high risk when stocks are selling at extremes of overvaluation based on their multiples of earnings, book value, and dividends, then the market will be at low risk when stocks are selling at low valuation levels based on the same criteria. We know that the S&P 500 was selling at roughly 29 times its earnings, 6 times its book value, and 70 times its dividend in late 1998, and that through the decades, on average, it trades at 14 times earnings, 1.6 times its book value, and 24 times its dividend.

We also know it's almost inevitable the market will decline at least to average valuation levels in bear markets. Therefore, by simply watching those valuation multiples decline, we can watch the bear market approach its bottom. *Barron's*, available at newsstands, includes the valuation multiples for all the major market indexes in each weekly issue.

PUBLIC PARTICIPATION ALSO SLINKS AWAY

Like Wall Street operators since stocks first began trading, we need to observe the public's attitude toward the stock market and recognize what it tells us about where the market is in its cycle.

We know that public investors tend to become interested in having their assets in the stock market only in the final stages of a bull market, after it has already made exciting gains. We know they then become fully trained to be buy and hold investors by the time the market reaches its top. We know they will therefore hold through the subsequent decline, even buying what they believe are just more temporary dips, ensuring that they will be fully invested throughout the decline.

And we know from history that they will then bail out in despair near the ultimate low, and be totally uninterested in the market, in fact unwilling to even discuss "the damned market" until the next bull market is well underway.

Like Wall Street operators, we can observe the change taking place.

We can see it as the investor sentiment numbers compiled by *Investors Intelligence, The American Association of Individual Investors*, and *Consensus Inc.*, discussed in an earlier chapter, decline from extremes of optimism near the market top toward the extremes of pessimism that will prevail at the eventual market bottom.

We can observe it as the flow of money into mutual funds slows and begins to reverse to outflow when savvy investors begin to lighten up and raise cash, and then the outflow begins to accelerate, and eventually becomes a panic.

PLAYING WITH OTHER PEOPLE'S MONEY

We know that Wall Street does all it can to keep investors in and still buying as the market declines. Studies of human nature give us another possible reason why public investors do not begin to exit to any degree until their portfolios are showing an actual loss.

Have you ever been to a race track or a casino and made a profit right off the bat? Suppose you started out with $500, and after a quick run of luck you have $1000. Those who study human behavior say you will then mentally separate "your" $500 from "their" $500, even though it's all your money now. Playing with "their" $500 rather than your own, you'll become more aggressive, moving from the $5 window to the $50 window, or from the $2 blackjack table to the $10 table, and go for broke with more speculative bets that have a bigger chance of losing, but will pay off big if you win. However, once you've lost "their" $500, you'll go back to being conservative again with your own $500.

The same phenomenon seems to occur in the stock market, and the phenomenon accentuates the reckless euphoria near market tops. By the time the market nears an important top, everyone is playing with the house's money, going for broke at the $50 window, betting on long shots, looking for the next Microsoft, doubling down with margin.

Comes the next bear market, and although not happy to see their "winnings" disappearing, most investors don't really begin to panic until they're no longer playing with winnings, but are seeing the losses eating into their original capital.

So at what level would we expect that panic to set in? If we look at some of the tables shown in earlier chapters we see that 85 percent of the money currently in the market entered just since 1994.

If we then look at a chart of the market since 1994, we can see that the average market investment probably has a cost

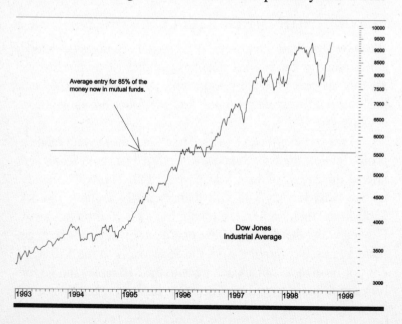

basis that correlates with a market around 5600 on the Dow. So, the real panic stage at the next bear market may not begin until a break below that level, when the average investor's losses have wiped out his or her winnings and are beginning to cut into his or her own capital.

However, behavioral analysts also tell us that we mentally move our winnings out of the "their money" box into the "our money" category with some regularity. In the situation of the casino or horse track gambler, their money becomes our money once we get it home, and it is our money when we next visit the casino or track. In the case of investors, the analysts believe most will consider their gains as winnings only until the gains show up on the next annual statement or tax return. Then it becomes "our money," and any erosion of it from that point will be an actual loss.

In any event, we will be looking for a panic stage as a sign the market is reaching a bear market low. If you look at the charts of previous bear markets that we have provided, you'll notice that in most there was an obvious panic collapse to the low. Technicians call that final plunge the capitulation stage, in which the majority of those still holding throw in the towel.

ANECDOTAL EVIDENCE

We'll also be very aware, as a bear market bottom approaches, that the euphoric excitement that prevails near a bull market top has reversed to absolute gloom and doom. And I'm not talking about increased worry or some degree of pessimism, such as seen at the bottom of the brief corrections of recent years. I'm talking about kick-the-dog, end-of-the-world despair. Bankruptcies will be soaring. Unemployment will be high. Consumer confidence will be very low. Wall Street will have forgotten all about telling you to buy and hold. They'll be telling you that the problems are too serious to end soon, that it's still too early to buy.

BEGIN TO BUY

But you will know when valuations have come down to fair value or below, based on the multiples of the S&P 500 to its earnings, book value, and dividends. You'll know when the public has pretty well panicked out, and when gloom and doom is the dominant theme in the media regarding not only the pitiful economy and sad excuse for a stock market, but even the outlook for the country's well-being.

Unlike those who are wringing their hands in despair over their growing losses, or those who have bailed out near the low and sworn off "the damned market" (never going to get sucked in again), you will have your profits, be sitting on cash, and just as important, will have confidence in yourself, in the market, and in the fact that you know how to stay on the right side of the cycle.

So, you should have the confidence to continue to ignore what Wall Street is telling you, as they work the propaganda now to keep the public out at the low prices until they have loaded up again. You can begin to accumulate good stocks from the bargain table.

You don't have to rush. The market won't run away from you on the upside even though it may seem at times to be doing so. Even if you hit the exact bottom, there will be almost as good second and third opportunities for good entries, as shown in the following chart.

In fact, market technicians will look for the market to "retest" the bottom, without breaking below it, as a confirmation that the low is in, and will do most of their buying after that successful retest. Another low-risk buying opportunity usually presents itself when the market breaks out above its long-term 200-day m.a. again. Until it does that, there is always the possibility the 200-day m.a. will act as overhead resistance on any rally attempts, causing the market to resume its decline. The risk diminishes considerably once the market is above its 200-day m.a., and more so once it has successfully retested the support at that moving average.

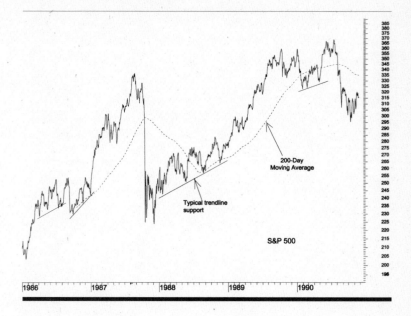

Another habit to get into is buying on weakness. That is, buy when the market pulls back to trendline or moving average support lines. That's the professional way. Most investors follow the opposite pattern. They'll be made optimistic after the market has rallied nicely off a support level and will continue to watch it rally to make sure it's a new trend, and then buy. It won't matter all that much if the market is undervalued and a bull market is just getting underway. However, gains will be enhanced if stocks are accumulated on pullbacks to support lines rather than after they've rallied for a while off those support lines.

Keep in mind that after bear markets have bottomed, when a new bull market is getting underway, you will be averaging into a low-risk market. This is the time to buy the dips and become an aggressive buy and hold investor, and remain so through the pullbacks and corrections, until the market again becomes overvalued and overbought, and the public has been enticed back in to dangerous levels of participation.

Enjoy.

ADDENDUM

What have we learned from our study of market history and analysis of the peculiar differences between the actions of Wall Street and that of most public investors?

- Bull markets train investors to believe this time is different and to disregard cycles.
- Bear markets come along more frequently than most investors realize and will devastate the portfolios of those who are not prepared.
- Bear markets can be harnessed to produce additional gains from the downside.
- Buy and hold investing is a badly flawed theory that does not work long term.
- Public investors have a history of buying high and selling low, whereas Wall Street takes the opposite side of those trades.
- Wall Street never has, and still does not, provide a level playing field.
- Wall Street's sole goal is profits for itself, even at the expense of its customers.
- The Seasonal Timing System almost tripled the market's gains on a buy and hold basis for at least the last thirty-five years, while cutting risk in half and eliminating most of the problems that make a buy and hold strategy so difficult to sustain.
- The next bear market is right around the corner and is liable to be a monster.

- Bear markets also end, and provide the investing opportunities of a lifetime.

What have I learned from writing this book?

Most books are written by those who already know pretty much all there is to know of a subject. I thought I was in that category when I began the project. How wrong I was.

I thought after a lifetime of dealing with brokerage firms, money managers, and mutual funds, including a number of years of running a money management firm, and the most recent twelve years researching and publishing an independent investment advisory service, that I knew all there is to know about the shenanigans of Wall Street. How disgusted I was to dig deeply into Securities and Exchange Commission and NASD filings and actions, the records of civil and criminal lawsuits, and other resources to learn how little has changed since the first securities were traded in 1790.

I was also dismayed to learn, but did not chronicle herein, that the move of the nation's banks into the brokerage industry in recent years has not cleaned the industry up, but merely broadened the ranks of those who insist on maximizing profits at the expense of the public.

On the positive side, I was delighted with what our research and development of the Seasonal Timing System accomplished. I had always been aware of the *tendency* for the market to be positive in various seasonal patterns and had used that awareness in the market timing, stock and mutual fund recommendations, and risk management advice in our newsletter. However, what we learned about seasonality as we proceeded with the research for *Riding the Bear*, has led, in 1999, to incorporating the Seasonal Timing System into our newsletter and ongoing work of timing the market.

INDEX

A

Adams, John, 144
Advice. *See also* Common sense; Risk management
 from brokers, 192, 198-199
 from company, 192
 from experts, 1-2, 17, 30-32, 41, 44, 47, 50, 64, 92, 93-94, 207
 independent research for, 193
 investigating, 188-191, 193-194
 performance claims as, 202-203
Amalgamated Copper, 166
American Association of Individual Investors, 105, 213
American Residential Services, 200
American Steel & Wire, 163-164
American Stock Exchange, Emerging Company Marketplace, 190-191
Anaconda Copper, 166
Appel, Gerald, 79
Asian recession
 effect on U.S., 139-140
 Hong Kong market collapse and, 11-13, **12**, **38-39**
Assembly line manufacturing, 3
Assets. *See also* Earnings multiples
 relation to valuation, 98-99
Assets allocation. *See also* Market capitalization
 in bull markets, 6, 22, 105, 132-**133**
 compared to GNP, 134-**135**
 investment discipline for, 124

B

Bad stocks. *See also* Good stocks
 investor demand for, 18-21
BankBoston, 112-114, **113**
Banking industry
 crisis in, 144-146
 in Japan, 10
Bankruptcy, 11, 207, 215
Barron's, 106, 187, 212
Baruch, Bernard, 51, 53, 162, 164-165, 170, 206
Baruch, My Own Story (Baruch), 165
Bass Brothers, 51
Bear markets. *See also* Stock market cycles
 average occurrence of, 1, **4**, 26, **137**, **156**-157, 211
 average declines in, 1, **4**, 154, 157, 167, 208-**209**
 capitulation stage in, **214**-215
 catalysts of, 25-26, 93, **95**
 duration of, 40, 111, 148, 154, 205
 effect on buy and hold investor, 33-34, 35-**36**, 195, 213-215, **214**

effect on individual stocks, 17-21, 151-152
 factors effecting, 15, 22-28
 historical record of, **4**
 indicators of, 105-107, 139-141, 147-158
 1968-1970, 210-**211**
 1973-1974, 208-**209**
 1987, **148**-149
 profile of, 3-4, 26-28, 142, 152-153
 profiting from, 45-46
 "retesting bottom," 216-**217**
 Seasonal Timing System and, 87-88
 speed of, compared to bull market, 87
 undervaluation levels in, **101**-102
Berkshire Hathaway, 51-53, 141
Bonds
 government, 160, 161
 interest rates and, 102
Book value. *See also* Overvaluation
 relation to valuation, 98-99, 157, 212, 216
Bounce, 150, 188
Brady bonds, 144
Brokerage firms. *See also* Securities fraud; Wall Street
 advice to investors, 1-2, 17, 30-32, 41, 44, 47, 50, 64, 92, 93-94
 bank and insurance involvement in, 145
 business practices of, 175-176
 commissions of, 196-198
 discount brokers, 192, 196-199
 growth of stock brokers, 133-134, 187
 market timing by, 48
 performance awards of, 203
 relations with investors, 58, 105, 176-177, 185-187, 191
 resources available from, 78, 192
Buffett, Warren, 3, 40, 141
 investment strategy of, 51-53
Bull markets. *See also* Overvaluation
 after 1929 crash, 208
 asset allocation in, 6, 22
 duration of, 92, 205
 effect on individual stocks, 17-21
 indicators of, 105-107, 217
 investor emotions in, 14-15
 speed of, compared to bear market, 87
 supply and demand forces in, 24
Business Week, 191
Buy and hold investors. *See also* Public investors
 bear market effecting, 27-28, 33-34, 35-**36**, 44, 148, 154, 168
 in contemporary market, 37-39, 64, 141, 206, 217
 psychology of, 15, 29, 30-33, 40-41, 195, 212-213

seasonality effecting, 61-62
Buy signals. *See also* Market timing
    MACD triggers for, **54-55**, 79, 80-82, **81-82**
    seasonality and, 60-61, 72-74
    unemployment rates and, 95-96
Buying opportunities, in bear market, 28, 205,
    208-**209**, 210-**211**, 216-217

C

California, real estate cycles in, 7-9
Canada, 140
Capital gains tax, 25-26
CDs. *See* Certificates of deposit
Certificates of deposit (CDs), interest rates and,
    68, 102, 183-184
Charles Schwab & Co., 177
Chrysler, **114**-115
Chrysler, Walter, 162, 189
Circuit City, 200
Common sense. *See also* Advice; Risk
    assessment
    in market timing, 72-74, **73**, 75
Communism, 6, 7
Computerized trading, 48, 149, 155, 199
Computers
    impact on productivity, 2, 43
    for market timing predictions, 78
    Y2K glitch, 146-147
Consensus Inc., 105, 213
Consumer confidence. *See also* Investor confi-
    dence
    economic indicators and, 143-144
    effect on market, 94-95, 96
    following Japanese stock market decline, 11
Consumer Price Index, 103
Continental Tobacco, 165
Corporate earnings. *See also* Earnings multiples;
    Price/earning ratios
    decline of, 27, 140, 143
    growth of, 2, 155
    interest rate hikes effecting, 25
    relation to stock price, 97-98
Corrections. *See also* Stock market cycles
    discussed, 108, 207
Cousins, Norman, 93
Credit cards, cash advances with, 132
Crosscurrents, 61

D

Danforth, William, 166, 206
Dean Witter Reynolds, 177
Derivatives trading, 145-146
Disney, 115-**116**
Dividends. *See also* Overvaluation
    market timing and, 68, 69
    relation to valuation, 10, **101**-102, 204, 216
Dow Jones Industrial Average (DJIA). *See also*
    Stock market cycles
    compared to 200-day moving average, **108**
    1910-1999, 206
    1915-1999, 30-**31**
    1960-1998, 35-**36**
    1967-1982, **34**
    1986-1989, **35**
    short term MACD indicator and, 78-**79**
    theory of restoration of, 42-44
    trendline of average gains, **156**-157, 217
    trendline overextension, 136-138, **137**

Dow Jones News/Retrieval, 115, 193
Drew, Daniel, 162
Drexel Burham Lambert, 184
Drexel, Morgan & Co., 164
Duke, James, 165

E

Earnings multiples. *See also* Corporate earnings;
    Overvaluation
    relation to valuation, 10, 98-99, 99-102, 136,
    206, 212, 216
Economy
    indicators for, 143
    structural changes in, 2
Electricity, economic impact of, 2-3, 155
Emerging Company Marketplace, 190-191
Entertainment stocks, 43
Equis International, Metastock Professional, 78
Excesses. *See also* Overvaluation
    in 1998 market, 147, 155-156
    role in bear market, 22-28, 126
Expectations
    investor euphoria and, 3
    mistakes and, 124
Experts. *See also* Advice; Brokerage firms
    advice to investors, 1-2, 17, 30-32, 41, 44, 64
    investigating advice from, 188-191

F

Farming and agriculture, 6
Fear. *See also* Investor confidence; Pessimism
    effect on investor psychology, 14-15, 168-169
    in market collapse, 150
Federal Reserve, 25, 133, 146, 150
    effect on stock market, 56-57, 157-158
Fidelity Latin America Fund, MACD trigger
    and, **54**
Fidelity Magellan Fund, 49, 201
Financial World, 178
Fisk, Jim, 162, 163
FitzGerald, Niall, 147
Florida Land Crash, 7
Flynn, John T., 172
Fosback, Norman, 46-47, 57, 60, 65
Futures contracts, mutual funds and, 91

G

Gates, Bill, 3
Gates, John W., 163
GDP. *See* Gross Domestic Product
General Motors stock, **97**
"Goldilocks" economy
    characteristics of, 2
    myths about, 154-158
Goldman Sachs, 177
Good stocks. *See also* Bad stocks
    in bear-market-type mutual funds, 92
    myths about, 195, 204
    1987 decline effecting, 151-152
    overvaluation of, 96-97
Gould, Edson, 56, 57
Graham, Benjamin, 53
Great Depression, 3, 34, 158, 207. *See also*
    1929 crash
Greed
    in banking industry, 144-146
    effect on investor psychology, 14-15, 208
Greenspan, Alan, 133, 140, 157

Gross Domestic Product (GDP), compared to market capitalization, 134-**135**, 138, **155**-156

H

Hamilton, Alexander, 159
Harriman, E.H., 169
Hirsch, Yale, 60, 61, 65
Hong Kong flu
    Asian recession and, 11-13, **12**, 38-**39**
    Hang Seng rise and collapse, **12**, **38**, **152**
Horizon Healthcare, 199-200

I

IMF. *See* International Monetary Fund
Income taxes, 14
Individual retirement accounts (IRAs), 178
Indonesia, 13, 143
Inflation
    effect on market, 93-95, 102-103
    Federal Reserve policies effecting, 25
Initial public offerings (IPOs), bull markets and, 24, 105
Insiders. *See also* Market timing; Securities
    fraud
    contemporary, 199-200
    investment strategies of, 50, 93, 140, 193, 195
    short selling stocks and, 111-115, 119
Insiders, The, 112, 200
Instinet, 199
Institute for Econometric Research, 60
Institutional investors, response to bear market, 26-27
Interest, on cash deposits, 68, 69
Interest rates, effect on market, 25, 56-57, 94-95, 102-103, 157
International Monetary Fund (IMF), bailout policies, 143
Investment advisers, 134. *See also* Advice; Brokerage firms; Experts
Investment clubs. *See also* Public investors
    growth of, 128-**129**
Investor confidence. *See also* Consumer confidence
    in bear market, 216-217
    of buy and hold investors, 37-39
    effect on stock prices, 18-21
Investor euphoria. *See also* Assets allocation
    in 1929 and 1990s, compared, 2-3
    indicators of, 6, 22, 134, 138
Investor psychology
    of buy and hold investor, 15-16
    effect on market movement, 13-14, 93-96
Investor sentiment. *See also* Public participation
    risk assessment and, 103-105, 213
Investors' Business Daily, 187
Investors Intelligence, 105, 107, 213
IPOs. *See* Initial public offerings
IRAs. *See* Individual retirement accounts

J

Japanese stock market
    Nikkei decline, 10-**11**
    rise and fall of, 9-11, 38-39, 136
Jones, Paul Tudor, 51

K

Keane, James R., 162, 164
Kennedy, John F., 25

Kennedy, Joseph P., 3, 51, 53, 162, 170, 189
    SEC appointment, 172-173
    stock manipulations by, 165-169, 206-207
KLM Airlines, 147

L

Latin America, 140
Lehman Brothers, 177
Leifer, Joel, 185
Leverage. *See also* Short selling
    margin debt and, 130-132, **131**, 203
    with put options, 123, 124
    in real estate transactions, 8, 9
Limited partnerships, 175, 197
    fraud and, 177-178, 178-182
Livermore, Jesse, 51, 104
Long position, 116
    mutual funds and, 92
    profit-taking and, 88, 89
Lynch, Peter, 40, 49, 116

M

MACD. *See* Moving Average Convergence Divergence
Malaysia, 13
Margin accounts, 117
Margin debt, investment levels and, 130-132, **131**
Market capitalization. *See also* Assets allocation; Savings
    compared to GDP, 134-**135**, 138, **155**-156
Market timing
    in bear market, 216-217
    by big-name investors, 51-53
    by brokerage firms, 48
    by corporate insiders, 50, 93
    expert advice about, 41, 47
    investment growth and, 46-48, 195
    market timing tools, 77-78
        short-term trend timing, 78-80, **79**
    Seasonal Timing System, 58-75, 80-82, 85, 86, 142, 210
        common sense and, 72-74, **73**, 75
        in declining market, 87-88
        monthly strength period, 65
        procedure for, 65-72, **66-67**, 74-75
    technical indicators, 53-56, **54**, **55**
        MACD indicators, 78-80, **79**, 80-82, **81-82**
        MACD results, 83-86, **83-85**
    "Two Tumbles and a Jump" system, 56-57
Market tops. *See* Stock market cycles
Market Vane, 105
Media, investment advice in, 47, 94, 141, 187
Medical science, 7
Merrill Lynch, 150, 177
Metastock Professional, 78
Mexico, stock exchange collapse, **153**
Micron Technology, 201-**202**
Mistakes, 116-117, 124
Monetary policy, effect on stock market, 56-57, 102-103, 143, 157
Money market accounts, interest rates and, 68, 102-103
Morgan, J.P., 51, 53, 162, 168
Moving Average Convergence Divergence (MACD). *See also* 200-day moving average
    market timing and, 53-56, **54**, **55**, 78-80, **79**
    results of using, **83-85**
Mutual funds

ABOUT THE AUTHOR

When he's not revealing the truth about Wall Street in book form, Sy Harding is the founder and CEO of Asset Management Research Corporation, and publishes its research in *Sy Harding's Street Smart Report*, an eight-page newsletter for professionals and serious investors.

Sy Harding's Street Smart Report is published every three weeks. A subscription includes a weekly interim telephone hotline update, and the option of viewing and printing the newsletter and hotlines instantly from a Web site on the Internet.

To subscribe to *Sy Harding's Street Smart Report*, call toll free 1-888-HARDING, or write to: Sy Harding's Street Smart Report, 169 Daniel Webster Highway, Suite 7, Meredith, NH, 03253-5614. Subscriptions are $225 per year, but are available to readers of *Riding the Bear* at the special rate of $195 per year.